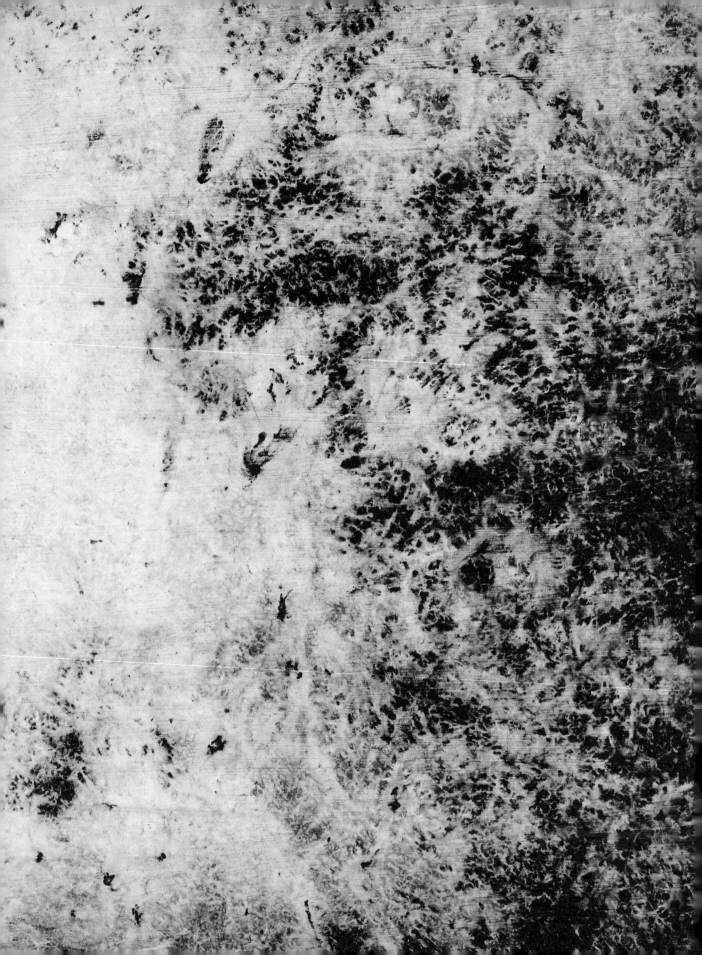

# DALMATIA

hardie grant books

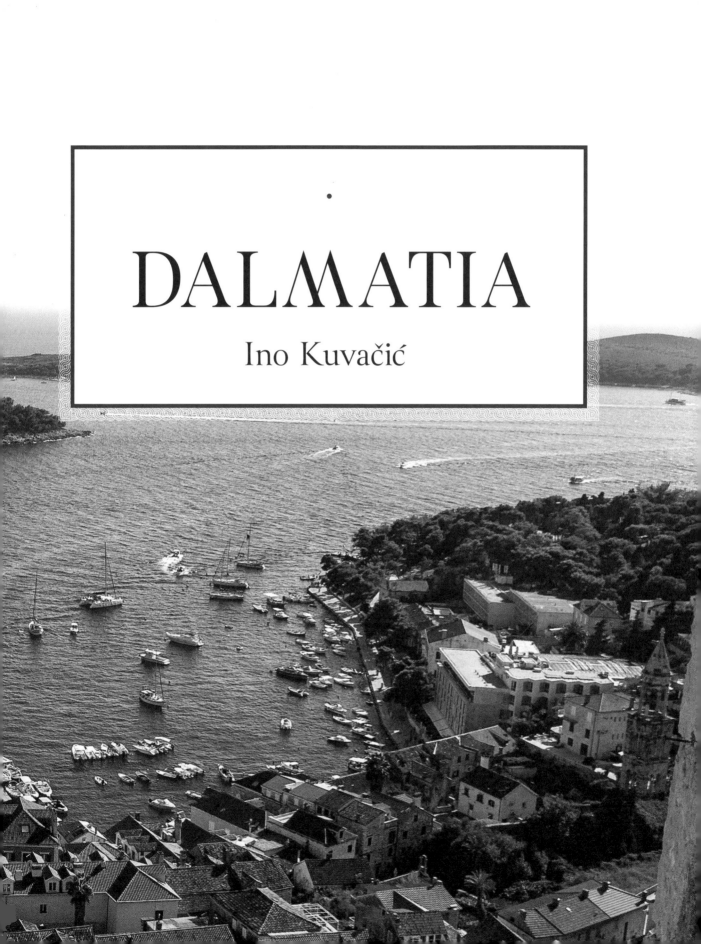

# DALMATIA

## Ino Kuvačić

# Introduction

•

I was born and raised in Split, Dalmatia's largest city, probably best known for the 4th century Roman emperor Diocletian's palace, which forms much of the city centre. I spent my childhood years living between the old family home in Split and our holiday house on the nearby island of Šolta.

My love and appreciation for food and wine runs deep – my maternal ancestors were one of the largest wine merchant families throughout the 18th and 19th centuries in coastal Croatia.

Some of my most profound childhood memories are of wine-making and olive-picking in my family's vineyards and olive groves. My father's ancestors were proud Croatian farmers, working the dry Dalmatian land, which consists mainly of rock and only a little soil. They weren't able to produce much, but what they lacked in quantity, they made up for in quality and flavour.

So many of the recipes in this book are dishes that I grew up eating and watching being prepared by my family, especially my grandmother Tomica and her sister Ljube. I've tried to stay as true as possible to them and if there's something I would like you to take away from this book, it's the feeling of honesty and warmth – and of course the importance of using produce of the highest available quality, which has always been the backbone of my cooking.

I hope you enjoy this journey through Dalmatia's cuisine and some of my own personal culinary memories.

*Ino Kuvačić*

# A rich tapestry of influences

Croatians consider themselves invariably lucky to come from such a beautiful country, with its pristine landscape and delicious variety of food and wine. Located in the heart of Europe, at the crossroads of many cultures and with a population of just over four million, it's become a huge tourist drawcard in recent years.

Thanks to Croatia's distinct geographic regions and influences resulting from a long and complex history, the cuisine has many variations. It is a country of regional cuisines, with a distinct divide between the southern coastal and northern continental culinary cultures.

This book focuses on the authentic food of the coastal region of Dalmatia. You'll notice that the recipes in this cookbook don't include as many herbs or spices as other cuisines – the key to Croatian cooking is fresh ingredients, grown in nutrient-rich, pure earth. The clean air, abundance of water in many parts of the country and different types of soils all over the region mean that the produce itself is some of the best in Europe. The inherent flavours of the vegetables, meat and fish lend themselves to simple yet refined recipes that warm the heart and soul.

## Threads of history

Croatia is a tiny country with extraordinary topographical diversity, bordered by Hungary, Slovenia, Serbia, Montenegro and Bosnia Herzegovina, also sharing a maritime border with Italy. As such, its culinary history has been shaped by its turbulent political history, influenced by the many different ethnic groups that either passed through, exerted power over or occupied the lands that are now Croatia. It has continuously absorbed and adapted the various cultural elements that have made their way through its territories, taking a little of everything to become its own unique blend. Predominantly Italian elements, with notes of French and hints of Turkish, are woven into the lean coastal cuisine (of Dalmatia, Istria and Primorje), comprising lots of vegetables, fish and seafood along with the mandatory olive oil. The north, on the other hand (Zagorje, Slavonija and Lika), has been shaped by Germanic, Austrian, Hungarian and Turkish strands. This cuisine is characterised by hearty meat, poultry, dairy products and starchy foods, rich desserts and pickles – a product of the rich and fertile land.

Dalmatia, the region that makes up most of the southern coast, has been heavily exposed to influences from around the Mediterranean, first being colonised by the Ancient Greeks and Romans, who brought wine-making to the region. Following the fall of these great civilisations, the Byzantines and Avars had a major impact on the region, along with the Croatian Kingdom between 925 and 1102. By the 11th century, Dalmatia had become

part of the Hungarian–Croatian kingdom and in 1409 Dalmatia was sold by King Ladislav to Venice, opening the region up to Renaissance culture and influence. However, there was an ever-growing feeling of Croatian cultural identity.

The eastern Ottoman Empire swept through the Balkans in the 1450s and, to this day, one can see the culinary impact in dishes such as ćevapčići (skinless sausages) and đuveđ (sautéed vegetables with rice). In 1797 Napoleon incorporated Dalmatia into his Illyrian Provinces, lending a heavy French influence to the region, which is evident in some of the dishes such as rožata, a kind of crème caramel.

In 1815, Dalmatia was incorporated into the Habsburg Empire and Italian became the official language. It was during this time that the Austrian and Hungarian cultures heavily influenced the area of today's Croatia. A lasting legacy were things like the expansion of coffee houses and cakes, such as the famous sacher torte.

With the fall of the Habsburgs in 1918, Dalmatia was claimed by both Italy for a period and the new Kingdom of Serbs, Croats and Slovenes. In 1945 after World War II, Yugoslavia became the overarching federation and much traditional farming of produce was neglected, instead taken over by heavy industry. After a period of unrest during the 1980s, following the death of President Tito, Croatia finally declared its independence in 1991.

Today, it seems that the hunger for growing local produce and reviving old trades is back with a vengeance. What is grown and produced now in the country is among the best in Europe, and locals and foreigners are becoming increasingly aware of this as they fall in love with Croatian cuisine all over again.

## Dalmatia and its cuisine

Dalmatia is a region defined by the sea, with white-pebbled beaches, azure blue sky and the myriad islands that sparkle like jewels in the crystal clear Adriatic. The climate is typical of the Mediterranean, as is the vegetation, with olive trees, lavender bushes, vineyards and fragrant pine trees. Vegetables and seafood are the staples of a diet that has had to do the best it could with harsh, rocky terrain. Dalmatians had to be frugal and inventive, creating the best they could with limited produce. Meat has always been a luxury and rich dishes were only ever served at festivities or during special times of the year, such as Christmas. Much like other Mediterranean diets though, this has been a blessing in disguise as the diet is healthy, as is evident in the traditionally low rates of diet-related illnesses. Vegetables such as silverbeet (Swiss chard), tomatoes, asparagus and beans are the cornerstone of the Dalmatian diet and feature heavily in the recipes in this book, along with the fresh harvest from the sea, such as sardines, octopus and mussels. And of course olives and grapes are like gems produced by the earth in this region, olive oil often being considered as 'liquid gold'.

More elaborate dishes that feature on the Dalmatian table include brudet (a thick fish soup, which is served with soft polenta), crni rižot (squid ink, or black, risotto), punjene paprike (stuffed capsicums/bell peppers) and salata od hobotnice (octopus salad). Special occasions call for more complex dishes, requiring hours of preparation, and include meat. Slow cooking is characteristic of celebratory dishes in this area – pašticada is a rich, slow-cooked beef cheek stew with a thick prune and tomato sauce, often served with gnocchi, while peka is a slow roast of meat, potatoes and vegetables, cooked in their own juices in a wood-fired oven under a bell-shaped cover.

Wine-making has been an important part of Croatian culture for thousands of years and, as with the cuisine, there are two main wine regions – continental and coastal. Despite being a tiny country, Croatia has over 300 geographically-defined wine-producing areas. People all over Croatia enjoy wine with their meals daily, and have done so for many centuries.

## A typical Croatian meal

So what does a typical Croatian meal look like? In many parts of the country, and similar to many other countries in Europe, when entertaining guests, meals often begin with plates of cured meats (pršut in the south, kulen in the north) and various types of cheese, pickled vegetables and bread. This will be accompanied by an aperitif, such as a brandy, followed by the first course, a bowl of warm soup – no matter what the weather.

Next will come either a meat dish, such as peka or pašticada, or a roast, with a particular favourite being lamb on the spit from the island of Pag or the mountainous region of Lika. Suckling pig on the spit or roast turkey are also popular dishes in various parts of the country, and meals are usually accompanied by salads, roast vegetables or, in the north, boiled pastry called mlinci. Fish dishes would also be served as a main course in Dalmatia, such as many of the recipes featured in this book.

No meal with guests is ever complete without sweets and cakes, which often contain seasonal fruits and nuts (plums, apples, apricots, cherries, walnuts and hazelnuts). Strudels (from the Germanic influence), cream cakes, dumplings (eaten throughout Central Europe) together with pancakes are traditional favourites.

There is one more thing that no Croatian meal is complete without – brandy and liqueurs. A typical start or end to any meal is sweet cherry brandy (maraschino), warm walnut brandy (orahovica), pear brandy (kruškovac), potent plum brandy (šljivovica) and herbal grass brandy (travarica).

## Croatian hospitality

If you've ever been to a Croatian's house, you will know that one thing is true – we're a hospitable nation. Gost ('guest') is an emotionally charged word and visitors are treated with something akin to reverence. This is perhaps one of the things that really sets Croatian hospitality apart. We love to make our guests feel at home, as comfortable as possible, and a major part of this is ensuring they are well fed. The definition of a catastrophe (or embarrassment) in Croatia is not having enough food to serve people, so at all times there must be food and drink in the home deemed 'worthy' of any unexpected guests that may drop by, even if it's just for a cup of coffee.

However, Sunday lunch is reserved for families, and the streets of Croatia's cities and towns empty out as people sit with their loved ones for this cherished, almost sacred, weekly meal.

Nothing says Sunday lunch like the smell of freshly cooked beef soup wafting down from apartments all over northern Croatia, while nothing spells a festivity like the sweet smell of deep-fried, sugared fritule escaping from someone's window.

At meal times, portions are generous and dishes are served on the table for everyone to help themselves, although the host will encourage and refill plates. While it's not considered an insult to turn down food, it's definitely seen as contributing to the communal spirit by participating in both eating and drinking. Meals in the home have been a focal point of Croatian tradition and history and even though there has been a notable increase in people eating out in recent times, the home-cooked meal will always hold a special place in the heart of Croatians. And the dishes in this cookbook reflect just that.

*Slavica Habjanovic*

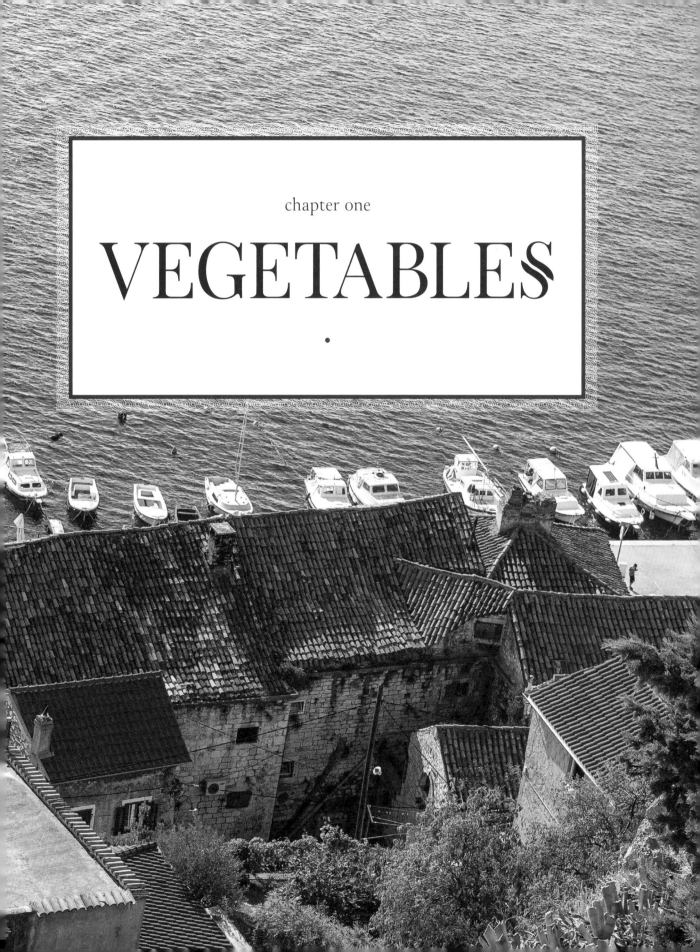

chapter one

# VEGETABLES

·

Even if meat or fish are the main dishes on the table, vegetables are always in the majority.

We truly love our vegetables in Croatia, and the diet in the coastal areas of the Mediterranean is rich with all kinds of fruit and vegetables. Even if meat or fish are the main dishes on the table, vegetables are always in the majority.

Every Dalmatian town has its own vegetable market, which is an integral part of everyday life. Generations of families visit the market to buy their daily food and to talk to their favourite local farmer – not just about which vegetables are in season and are the best quality, but also about the important subjects – politics, health, the weather, fashion and how many tourists there are in town this year.

'Spiza' is the Dalmatian word for food shopping. This activity has evolved through the centuries into almost a ritual; a celebration of everyday life. I love visiting Stari Pazar, the 'old market', in my hometown, Split. As well as a huge array of vegetables, there is a great pastry shop serving coffee with cream and the best vanilla slices.

The most popular vegetable in Dalmatia must be silverbeet (Swiss chard). Eaten mostly for dinner, silverbeet is often cooked with good-quality olive oil, garlic and potatoes and served with some protein – usually small fried fish or hard-boiled eggs. It makes a great light dinner with some good Dalmatian red wine.

Since being brought to Europe from the Americas in the 16th century, the potato has become a staple food in Croatian cooking. Almost all meals, except breakfast, will contain potatoes in some form or other.

Tomatoes, zucchini (courgettes) and eggplants (aubergines) are the most popular vegetables during the summer months, when they are in season, and are cooked in many different ways or prepared in salads.

# Carrot, capsicum and eggplant soup

*Juha od mrkve, balancana i crvene paprike*

SERVES 4

100 ml (3½ fl oz) extra-virgin olive oil

2 garlic cloves, crushed

1 large brown onion, chopped

200 g (7 oz) carrots, sliced

200 g (7 oz) red capsicums (bell peppers), washed and diced into 1 cm (½ in) pieces

200 g (7 oz) eggplant (aubergine), peeled and cut into 2 cm (¾ in) dice

1.2 litres (41 fl oz) vegetable stock

sea salt

freshly ground black pepper

fresh herbs, to garnish (optional)

•

**There is nothing better than starting a meal with a great soup. This is one of my favourite vegetable soups and I make it frequently in my restaurant as well as at home. Carrot, eggplant and capsicum complement each other very well. The soup can be served chilled, straight from the refrigerator, in summer months or piping hot from the stove in winter. Soups are always better served the day after making them, as this allows the flavours to develop.**

Put 30 ml (1 fl oz) of the olive oil in a large saucepan over high heat. Add the garlic and fry for just a few seconds until it releases its aroma, making sure it doesn't start to colour. Add the onion and sauté for 10 minutes over medium heat until translucent. Add the carrot and sauté for another 10 minutes.

In a separate frying pan, heat another 30 ml (1 fl oz) of the olive oil and sauté the capsicum until it starts to become a nice golden-brown colour. Season with salt and pepper then add it to the saucepan with the carrot mixture.

Add another 30 ml (1 fl oz) olive oil to the empty saucepan and sauté the eggplant until it starts to colour and soften. Season with salt and pepper then add it to the saucepan with the carrot and capsicum mixture.

Add the vegetable stock to the saucepan with the vegetables and bring to the boil. Lower the heat and simmer for about 15–20 minutes, until the vegetables are soft and start to break up.

Purée the mixture in the saucepan using a hand-held blender until smooth. Adjust the seasoning, drizzle with the remaining olive oil and serve, garnished with fresh herbs if desired.

# Sour cherry soup

*Juha od maraske*

1 kg (2 lb 3 oz) sour (morello) cherries, washed and pitted

150 g (5½ oz) caster (superfine) sugar

300 ml (10 fl oz/1¼ cups) red wine

1 cinnamon stick

4 cloves

300 ml (10 fl oz/1¼ cups) pouring (single/light) cream

sea salt

•

**The town of Zadar is famous for its maraska cherries and its Maraska Liqueur Company. You will probably have heard of maraschino liqueur, which is used all over the world and made in many countries. However, the original cherry liqueur comes from the Croatian town of Zadar.**

Reserving 20 whole cherries for the garnish, place the remaining cherries, sugar, 500 ml (17 fl oz/2 cups) water, the red wine, cinnamon stick and cloves in a large saucepan. Bring to the boil and cook for 5–10 minutes over medium heat.

Add the cream and cook for another 5 minutes over medium heat. Season with salt. Discard the cinnamon stick and cloves.

Purée the soup with a hand-held blender until smooth. Stir in the whole pitted cherries.

Chill the soup in the refrigerator for a couple of hours, then serve with toasted bread.

# Stuffed bread from Vis

*Viška pogača*

SERVES 4

FILLING

80 ml ($2\frac{1}{2}$ fl oz/$\frac{1}{3}$ cup) olive oil

6 brown onions, thinly sliced

6 large tomatoes, cut into 1 cm ($\frac{1}{2}$ in) cubes

3 tablespoons chopped flat-leaf (Italian) parsley

100 g ($3\frac{1}{2}$ oz) anchovies, chopped

sea salt

freshly ground black pepper

DOUGH

500 g (1 lb 2 oz/$3\frac{1}{3}$ cups) plain (all-purpose) flour

10 g ($\frac{1}{4}$ oz) fresh yeast

10 g ($\frac{1}{4}$ oz) salt

80 ml ($2\frac{1}{2}$ fl oz/$\frac{1}{3}$ cup) olive oil

**Vis is an ancient island in the Adriatic Sea. It was founded in 397 BC by the ancient Greeks from Syracuse, which is known today as southern Sicily. Viška pogača actually resembles some Sicilian dishes cooked today. I can imagine that this savoury treat was made in a similar way 2400 years ago – except with no tomato, as that was only introduced to Europe in the 17th century. In the Vis town of Komiža, this pastry is often still prepared the ancient way without tomato, but with the addition of olives.**

For the filling, heat the oil in a frying pan over medium heat and sauté the onions for 10 minutes until translucent. Add the tomatoes and season with salt and pepper, then cook for 20 minutes. Remove from the heat, allow to cool then stir in the parsley and anchovies. Set aside.

For the dough, put the flour, 300 ml (10½ fl oz) water, yeast and salt in a stand mixer – or in a bowl if you are using a hand mixer. On medium speed work the dough for about 20 minutes, then add the olive oil and work for a further 5 minutes until the mixture comes together. Put the dough in a greased container and cover with a clean cloth or plastic wrap. Let the dough stand in a warm spot (22–28°C/72–82°F) until it doubles in size, about 30–40 minutes.

Grease a 20 cm (8 in) baking tray. Divide the dough in two. Roll out the first piece of dough to a thickness of 1.5 cm (⅝ in) and the dimensions of your baking tray, allowing for an extra 1 cm (½ in) of overhang all around. Lay the piece of dough on the baking tray, leaving the extra 1 cm of dough overhanging the tray. Spread the anchovy filling on top of the dough.

Roll out the second piece of dough the same way, then use it to cover the first piece of dough. Twist the edges to seal the dough, prick with a fork and let it sit for 20–25 minutes in a warm place.

Preheat the oven to 180°C (350°F).

Before baking, brush the top of the dough with water and sprinkle with salt. Bake in the oven for 25–30 minutes or until golden brown. When baked, cover the pogača with a clean cloth and leave it to cool, then cut it into squares or triangles and serve.

# Eggs and tomatoes
## *Jaja i pome*

SERVES 4

50 ml (1¾ fl oz) extra-
virgin olive oil

150 g (5½ oz) brown
onions, sliced into 5 mm
(¼ in) thick slices

400 g (14 oz) tomatoes,
cut into 1.5 cm (½ in) dice

4 eggs

sea salt

freshly ground black
pepper

1 tablespoon chopped
flat-leaf (Italian) parsley,
to garnish

**This is the perfect summer snack to eat after waking from an afternoon siesta. It might not look very beautiful, but it's delicious and refreshing eaten either hot or cold. The flavours work together really well.**

Put the olive oil and onion in a large saucepan over high heat and sauté for about 2 minutes (the onion doesn't need to soften). Add the tomato and cook for 10 minutes, until the sauce thickens a little.

Remove the pan from the heat and add the eggs, stirring them through. Cook for another couple of minutes over low heat until the eggs are cooked. Season with salt and pepper to taste, sprinkle with the parsley and serve.

# Baked black olives

*Pečene masline*

MAKES 1 KG (2 LB 3 OZ)

100 g (3½ oz) salt for the jar, plus 2 tablespoons extra

1 kg (2 lb 3 oz) fresh large, round black olives (select nice-looking ones), washed

50 ml (1¾ fl oz) extra-virgin olive oil

rosemary or thyme sprigs

•

**This recipe is very simple and is a great way to preserve olives. I love olives prepared like this – they are slightly bitter and tangy in flavour and they keep for a long time without any chemicals or preservatives. My family has a small olive grove on the island of Šolta in Croatia. When I was young, this was our favourite way to enjoy olives all year round.**

In a saucepan, bring 2 litres (68 fl oz/8 cups) water and the salt to the boil. Turn off the heat, add the olives and let them sit in the hot water for about 20 minutes.

Preheat the oven to 200°C (400°F). Line a baking tray with baking paper.

Drain the olives and dry them with a clean tea towel (dish towel). Transfer the olives to the baking tray and bake in the oven for 20 minutes. They are ready when they start to wrinkle. Remove the olives from the oven and leave to cool on the tray.

Transfer the olives to a large sterilised glass jar or several smaller ones. Top the jar with some thyme or rosemary and sprinkle with the olive oil and the extra 2 tablespoons salt. Shake the jar and seal it. The olives will keep for several months sealed. Once opened, keep them refrigerated and eat within a week.

# Artichokes Dalmatian-style
## *Artičoke na dalmatinski*

SERVES 4

8 artichokes

juice of 1 lemon

200 g (7 oz) fresh peas

200 g (7 oz) fresh broad (fava) beans, podded

400 ml (13½ fl oz) vegetable stock

100 ml (3½ fl oz) white wine

sea salt

freshly ground black pepper

2 tablespoons chopped flat-leaf (Italian) parsley, to garnish

FILLING

100 g (3½ oz/1 cup) dry breadcrumbs

150 ml (5 fl oz) extra-virgin olive oil

2 garlic cloves, chopped

2 anchovies, chopped

**This is a great recipe to discover the enchanting, earthy flavour of the artichoke. The outer leaves of artichokes are full of fibre and aren't edible, but there is a small amount of succulent flesh on the bottom of the inner leaves – don't waste this flesh as it's pure heaven. To eat the artichokes, enjoy every bit of the leaf by putting it in your mouth and sucking the delicious flesh.**

Clean the artichokes by cutting the stems 1 cm (½ in) from the bottom. Shave off the skin of the artichoke stem, then cut about 1 cm (½ in) off the top of the artichoke. Peel off one layer of the outer leaves.

Blanch the artichokes in simmering seasoned water with half the lemon juice for about 5 minutes. Drain. Leave the artichokes to cool while you prepare the filling.

For the filling, put the breadcrumbs in a bowl with 100 ml (3½ fl oz) of the olive oil, the garlic, anchovies and the remaining lemon juice. Season with salt and pepper. Mix well then push the breadcrumb mixture into the tops of the artichokes.

Place all the stuffed artichokes, facing up, in a large saucepan along with the fresh peas and broad beans. Add the vegetable stock and white wine. Ensure the artichokes are not covered with the stock, just submerged halfway. Season well, cover with a lid, and simmer for 40–50 minutes over low heat.

When cooked, sprinkle the artichokes with the parsley and remaining extra-virgin olive oil and serve with the peas and broad beans.

# Cabbage with pasta sheets

*Krpice sa zeljem*

SERVES 4

sea salt
freshly ground black
pepper

PASTA

500 g (1 lb 2 oz/6⅔ cups)
plain (all-purpose) flour
or 00 flour
5 eggs
1 teaspoon salt
1 tablespoon extra-virgin
olive oil

CABBAGE

50 ml (1¾ fl oz) olive oil
1 tablespoon sugar
1 brown onion, chopped
½ large green cabbage,
shredded

**This dish is known in Croatia as 'little clothes', as this is what the broken pieces of pasta resemble. Krpice can be served with any kind of meat, barbecued, poached or roasted – I love eating it with grilled chicken. As well as being served as a side dish, krpice is also nice as a starter or vegetarian main course. You can use pre-made pasta if you don't have time to make your own. Cabbage and pasta work like magic together and it's easy to get addicted, so beware.**

If you are making the pasta by hand, place the flour on a board or work surface. Make a well in the centre of the flour.

Crack the eggs into a bowl and whisk them with a fork. Add the salt and olive oil. Beat the mixture with a fork until smooth. Pour the egg mixture into the well in the flour and, using the tips of your fingers, mix the eggs into the flour, incorporating a little at a time, until everything is combined. Bring the mixture together into a ball.

You can also make the dough in a food processor. Put all the ingredients in the food processor and pulse until the mixture resembles breadcrumbs. Tip the mixture onto a board or work surface and bring it together into a ball.

Once you have your ball of dough, knead and work it with your hands to develop the gluten for about 5–10 minutes – otherwise your pasta will be soft when you cook it, instead of springy and al dente. Wrap the dough in plastic wrap and place it in the refrigerator to rest for about 30 minutes.

Once the pasta has rested, cut it into four pieces and roll each piece out with a pasta machine, starting with the widest setting and slowly working it to a 2 mm (1/16 in) thickness, or the second-last setting on the pasta machine. Sprinkle the pasta and the pasta machine with flour occasionally to prevent the dough from sticking and breaking. (You can roll the dough with a rolling pin if you don't have a pasta machine.) Once your pasta has been rolled into sheets, cut it into 1.5 cm (½ in) squares.

For the cabbage, put the olive oil and sugar in a saucepan and cook, stirring, until the sugar starts to brown and caramelise. Add the onion, season with salt and sauté until the onion is translucent. Add the cabbage and sauté for 20–25 minutes. Season with salt and pepper.

Cook the pasta in boiling salted water for about 5 minutes, drain well, add it to the cabbage and mix to combine. Add a little more olive oil. Adjust the seasoning and serve.

# Dalmatian mushrooms

*Gljive na brački način*

SERVES 6–8

2 kg (4 lb 6 oz) mushrooms (field or slippery jacks/sticky bun)

5 garlic cloves, crushed

250 ml (8½ fl oz/1 cup) extra-virgin olive oil

1 kg (2 lb 3 oz) brown onions, thinly sliced

100 ml (3½ fl oz) red wine vinegar

1½ tablespoons sugar

100 ml (3½ fl oz) prošek (Dalmatian fortified wine) or port

100 ml (3½ fl oz) Varenik (see below)

2 tablespoons tomato paste (concentrated purée)

sea salt

freshly ground black pepper

½ bunch flat-leaf (Italian) parsley, chopped, to garnish

VARENIK

5 kg (11 lb) red grapes

•

When olives are harvested in Dalmatia, usually in November, under the trees we always find lots of large mushrooms that we call pečurve. This recipe is a very traditional way of cooking these mushrooms and it makes a great lunch for cool autumn days. You can also use other kinds of mushrooms for this recipe. It is delicious served with pilaf rice.

In the old days before refined white sugar, varenik, or grape molasses, was used as a sweetener in Croatia. It is simple to prepare as it only has one ingredient. The flavour is truly unique with hints of caramel, fresh fruit, flowers and coffee. When I make a batch it lasts me a long time, and I add it to salads, sauces, stews and sometimes soups.

For the varenik, pick the grapes from the stems. Put the grapes through a fruit juicer then strain the juice through a fine-mesh sieve. Put the juice in a large saucepan over high heat and cook until it reduces to one tenth of its original volume, or until the juice becomes a syrup and starts to foam. You should have about 500 ml (17 fl oz/2 cups) of varenik. Allow to cool.

Clean the dust and soil from the mushrooms with a brush, then cut them into 1 cm (½ in) thick slices.

In a heavy-based pan, sauté the garlic in the olive oil over high heat for a few seconds, then add the onion. Season with salt and pepper, cover and sauté over low heat for 20 minutes, stirring occasionally, until the onion is translucent and you have a thick paste.

Add the sliced mushrooms, cover and sauté for a further 30 minutes until the mixture thickens.

In a bowl, mix the red wine vinegar with the sugar and 100 ml (3½ fl oz) water, stirring until the sugar has dissolved. Add this syrup to the pan, along with the prošek, varenik and tomato paste. Slowly braise, stirring occasionally, for about 2 hours or until the stew thickens. Garnish with the parsley, then serve.

# Goat's cheese crêpes with roast capsicum salsa

*Palačinke s kozjim sirom*

**In Croatia, palačinke, or crêpes, are one of the most loved dishes. They can be filled with savoury or sweet fillings and eaten as a starter, main or dessert. This dish is very easy to make, but you need to use good-quality goat's cheese. It makes a delicious appetiser to serve before a main meal.**

To make the crêpes, whisk the eggs in a large bowl. Add the milk, salt and 2 tablespoons of oil and mix well. Add the flour and mix vigorously until the batter is nice and smooth. Gently mix in the mineral water. Rest in the refrigerator for 15 minutes.

For the filling, gently mix all the ingredients together in a bowl.

For the salsa, combine all the ingredients in another bowl and season to taste with salt and pepper.

Cook the crêpes in a hot, non-stick 25 cm (10 in) frying pan. For each crêpe, pour in a little of the olive oil to grease the pan. Then pour in enough batter to cover the base of the pan, so the crêpes are around 2 mm (⅛ in) thick.

Place two crêpes on a sheet of plastic wrap (the crêpes should overlap each other by half). Spread the goat's cheese filling in a 1 cm (½ in) thick layer over the crêpes then roll the crêpes up, making sure they are tightly sealed in the plastic wrap. Refrigerate for 1 hour.

Preheat the oven to 190°C (375°F) and grease a baking dish.

Remove the plastic wrap from the crêpes but keep them rolled up, then cut them into 3 cm (1¼ in) slices. Place the crêpe slices in the prepared dish and bake in the oven for 5–10 minutes until golden brown. Serve in the baking dish or on a plate, and top with the roast capsicum salsa.

SERVES 4

CRÊPES

3 eggs

500 ml (17 fl oz/2 cups) milk

pinch of sea salt

2 tablespoons vegetable oil, plus 100 ml (3½ fl oz) extra, for frying

250 g (9 oz/1⅔ cups) plain (all-purpose) flour

250 ml (8½ fl oz/1 cup) sparkling mineral water

FILLING

600 g (1 lb 5 oz) soft goat's cheese, such as chèvre

2 eggs

pinch of freshly grated nutmeg

ROAST CAPSICUM SALSA

2 red capsicums (bell peppers), roasted, peeled and very finely diced

2 tablespoons capers

½ teaspoon chopped garlic

1 tablespoon chopped flat-leaf (Italian) parsley

1 tablespoon chopped thyme

2 tablespoons red wine vinegar

2 tablespoons Varenik (see page 35)

4 tablespoons extra-virgin olive oil

sea salt

freshly ground black pepper

# Zucchini fritters
*Fritule od tikvica*

SERVES 4–6

3–4 zucchini (courgettes)
1 red onion, finely
chopped
1 egg
handful dry breadcrumbs
50 g (1¾ oz) plain
(all-purpose) flour
vegetable oil, for
shallow-frying
sea salt
freshly ground black
pepper

**This is one of my favourite dishes in the warmer months. When I was a child we used to have this for lunch before heading to the beach. My childhood memories are coloured by the bright blues and greens of the Croatian summer – the intense turquoise of the Adriatic Sea and the jewel green of the pine trees and our vegetable garden. Every time I eat zucchini fritters my mind is filled with the memory of these colours and the joys of summer.**

Grate the zucchini, season it with salt and put it in a colander set over a shallow plate or bowl. Place a plate on top of the grated zucchini and then something heavy on top of the plate to press the water out of the mixture.

Leave the zucchini in the refrigerator for a couple of hours, then remove and squeeze out any excess liquid with clean hands.

Transfer the zucchini to a mixing bowl. Add the onion, egg, breadcrumbs and flour and mix well to combine. Season with salt and pepper to taste.

Shape the mixture into small patties with your hands. They can be palm-sized – or whatever size you like.

Heat some vegetable oil in a frying pan over medium heat and cook the patties until they are golden brown. Drain on paper towel then serve hot.

# Dalmatian silverbeet

*Blitva na dalmatinski*

SERVES 4

200 ml (7 fl oz) vegetable
stock or water

100 g (3½ oz) floury
potatoes, such as coliban
or king edward, sliced
1 cm (½ in) thick

200 g (7 oz) silverbeet
(Swiss chard)

4 garlic cloves, chopped

100 ml (3½ fl oz) extra-
virgin olive oil

sea salt

freshly ground black
pepper

•

**This is a staple in Dalmatia. Other Croatians actually call Dalmatians 'silverbeets' as we eat the vegetable almost every day – usually for dinner with some protein, hard-boiled eggs or fried fish. My wife and I sometimes use sweet potatoes in this recipe instead of regular potatoes.**

In a saucepan, bring the vegetable stock or water to the boil. Add the potatoes and cook for 10 minutes. Add the silverbeet, garlic, half the olive oil and season with salt and pepper. Cook for another 5–10 minutes then drain out most of the water – leave a little as the mixture needs to remain quite moist. Drizzle over the remaining olive oil and serve.

# Pastry stuffed with silverbeet
## *Soparnik*

SERVES 6–8

4 garlic cloves, finely chopped or crushed

100 ml (3½ fl oz) extra-virgin olive oil

sea salt

FILLING

1 kg (2 lb 3 oz) silverbeet (Swiss chard)

1 bunch flat-leaf (Italian) parsley

1 bunch spring onions (scallions), chopped

DOUGH

500 g (1 lb 2 oz/3⅓ cups) plain (all-purpose) flour

3 tablespoons extra-virgin olive oil

½ teaspoon salt

**Soparnik is a dish that is actually a protected cultural heritage item from Poljica, a region between the towns of Split and Omis in Dalmatia. Almost all of my ancestors are from that region. My grandmother gave me her soparnik recipe, which she used to make for special occasions. My task was to crush the garlic with the mortar and pestle and my grandfather was in charge of cutting the soparnik into perfect diamond-shaped pieces after it was cooked.**

For the filling, wash and dry the silverbeet, remove all the stems and cut the leaves into small strips. Wash and dry the parsley then chop it. Put all the filling ingredients in a bowl and season with salt. Set aside.

For the dough, put the flour in a large bowl, make a well in the centre and add the olive oil, salt and 250 ml (8½ fl oz/1 cup) water. Mix by hand (or with an electric mixer fitted with the dough hook) until you have a smooth dough. Allow the dough to rest in the refrigerator for about 30 minutes.

Preheat the oven to 200°C (400°F) and grease a baking tray.

Divide the dough in half and roll out each piece on a work surface dusted with flour to a thickness of about 1 mm (¹⁄₁₆ in) and about the size of your baking tray.

Spread one piece of the dough on the baking tray and cover it with the silverbeet mixture. Gently top with the other piece of dough. Seal the edges and prick the dough all over with a fork. Bake for about 20 minutes until the dough is cooked through and a nice golden colour.

When the soparnik is cooked, mix together the crushed garlic and olive oil and brush this mixture generously over the soparnik. Cut the pastry into 10 cm (4 in) diamond shapes and serve.

# Sautéed vegetables with rice

*Đuveđ*

SERVES 8–10

200 ml (7 fl oz) extra-
virgin olive oil

5 garlic cloves, crushed

500 g (1 lb 2 oz) red
onions, chopped

500 g (1 lb 2 oz) yellow
capsicums (bell peppers),
chopped into 1 cm ($\frac{1}{2}$ in)
cubes

500 g (1 lb 2 oz) crushed
tomatoes

2 tablespoons tomato
paste (concentrated
purée)

4 bay leaves

a few sprigs of oregano,
rosemary and thyme,
chopped

500 g (1 lb 2 oz) zucchini
(courgettes), chopped into
1 cm ($\frac{1}{2}$ in) cubes

500 g (1 lb 2 oz) eggplant
(aubergine), chopped into
1 cm ($\frac{1}{2}$ in) cubes

2 teaspoons sugar

200 g (7 oz) short-grain
white rice

sea salt

freshly ground black
pepper

**Turkish or Middle Eastern in origin, this dish is very popular in Croatia and is usually served with barbecued meats. However, it can also be eaten on its own and served hot or cold. Some people make đuveđ without rice during the summer months and preserve it in glass jars to enjoy it all year round, as it keeps for many months.**

Put half the olive oil and the garlic in a saucepan over high heat and cook the garlic for just a few seconds. Add the onion and sauté until soft, about 10 minutes. Add the capsicum and cook until soft, another 5 minutes, then add the crushed tomatoes, tomato paste, bay leaves and fresh herbs. Cook for about 10 minutes.

Put 50 ml (1¾ fl oz) of the remaining olive oil in a separate pan over high heat and sauté the zucchini until nice and golden brown, but do not let it get soft. Season with salt. Add the zucchini to the saucepan with the cooked capsicum and onion. Repeat the procedure with the eggplant. Add the sugar and adjust the seasoning. Remove from the heat.

Cook the rice in seasoned boiling water for 10 minutes – it should still have some bite.

Mix the rice into the vegetables in the saucepan, cover and let it rest for 30 minutes before serving.

# Wild asparagus with eggs and truffles
*Šparoge s jajima i istarskim tartufima*

SERVES 4

400 g (14 oz) wild or
regular asparagus

3 spring onions
(scallions), sliced

50 g (1¾ oz) unsalted
butter

8 eggs

50 ml (1¾ fl oz) thickened
(whipping) cream

20 g (¾ oz) black truffle
or 1 tablespoon black
truffle paste

sea salt

freshly ground black
pepper

•

**Wild asparagus is thinner and more pungent in flavour than regular asparagus. As spring awakes, wild asparagus start to appear in pine forests all over the Croatian coast. These vegetables have a magical flavour when cooked with eggs and, if you add some Istrian truffles, you will have a very special experience – a meal fit for the gods, as we say.**

Wash the asparagus and remove the woody ends – to do this, hold the bottom of the stem and gently bend the spear until the woody end snaps off.

Put the asaparagus, spring onion and butter in a non-stick frying pan over medium heat and sauté for 5 minutes.

Crack the eggs into a bowl and mix in the cream. Season with salt. If you are using truffle paste, add it now. Add the egg mixture to the frying pan and cook, mixing gently with a spatula until the eggs are cooked to your liking.

Divide the asparagus between the serving plates and top with some of the egg. If you are adding fresh truffle, shave some over the egg now. Sprinkle with a little pepper and serve hot.

# Sauerkraut

*Kiseli kupus*

MAKES 1 KG (2 LB 3 OZ)

1 kg (2 lb 3 oz) green
cabbage, shredded
1 carrot, grated
2 tablespoons polenta
50 g (1¾ oz) salt
1 tablespoon cumin or
fennel seeds

•

Sauerkraut is very popular throughout Central Europe and there are hundreds of recipes for it. It can be braised, eaten raw with salads, cooked with sausages or used in hearty soups. These days, sauerkraut and other fermented foods are regarded as superfoods and you can buy fancy sauerkraut in organic shops. It is easy to prepare yourself – unless your Croatian family, like mine, prepares 50 kg (110 lb) by hand, and then it's hard work! Every year my father makes his own sauerkraut in a huge barrel.

Mix all the ingredients together in a large bowl until well combined.

Begin transferring the mixture to a large, sterilised glass or plastic jar one handful at a time. After each layer of cabbage, press down on it with your fist until the liquid is released and comes to the top.

Keep adding the cabbage, continuing to press after each addition so all the liquid ends up at the top of the jar. When all of the cabbage is pressed in the jar, cover the jar with plastic wrap and seal the top with a lid to ensure it is airtight. Store in a cool, dark place for 40 days. After opening, eat the sauerkraut within a few weeks.

# Croatian potatoes

*Restani krumpir*

SERVES 4

1 kg (2 lb 3 oz) whole
waxy potatoes, such as
desiree, sebago or nicola,
with their skins left on

200 g (7 oz) brown onion,
thinly sliced

100 ml (3½ fl oz) extra-
virgin olive oil

2 tablespoons chopped
flat-leaf (Italian) parsley

sea salt

freshly ground black
pepper

•

**This is a great side dish to complement meat. Make sure you cook the
potatoes in their skins as this imparts a wonderful nutty flavour to the
dish. When you boil root vegetables like carrots, beetroot (beets) or
potatoes, you should always put them into cold water seasoned with salt
and then heat the pan. They will cook faster and more evenly this way.**

Put the potatoes in a saucepan of cold water and bring to the boil. Cook for
20–30 minutes (depending on the size of the potatoes) until soft. Let them
cool for 15 minutes, then peel and slice them 1 cm (½ in) thick.

Preheat the oven to 180°C (350°F).

In a saucepan over high heat, sauté the onion in the olive oil until soft
and golden brown, 10–15 minutes. Add the sliced potatoes, season well
with salt and pepper, mix well, then transfer to a baking dish.

Bake for 20–30 minutes. Sprinkle with the parsley and serve in the
baking dish.

# Eggplant, potato and tomato bake

*Melancane, krumpir i pomidori zapečeni*

SERVES 4–6

4 large eggplants (aubergines)

4 large floury potatoes, such as coliban or king edward

4 large ripe tomatoes

2 garlic cloves, crushed

1 large brown onion, chopped

100 ml (3½ fl oz) extra-virgin olive oil

250 ml (8½ fl oz/1 cup) vegetable stock

2 tablespoons chopped flat-leaf (Italian) parsley, to garnish (optional)

sea salt

freshly ground black pepper

•

**This dish is usually prepared during the day in summer then served cold at dinner. If you make it in winter, serve it hot. This bake can be served alongside barbecued fish or meat. Use a clay baking dish if possible as this will give the bake a better texture and flavour.**

Prick the eggplants with a fork and soak them in water for a couple of hours to reduce some of the bitterness. Peel the eggplants and cut them into 5 mm (¼ in) thick slices.

Peel the potatoes and cut them into 5 mm (¼ in) thick slices. Slice the tomatoes the same way.

In a saucepan over high heat, sauté the garlic and onion in 80 ml (2½ fl oz/⅓ cup) of the olive oil until translucent and just starting to colour. Season with salt.

Preheat the oven to 180°C (350°F).

Grease a baking dish with olive oil and start placing the vegetables in layers. Layer the vegetables (ensuring you start and finish with a layer of tomatoes), adding sautéed onion, garlic and seasoning to each layer. (You should end up with two to four layers of each vegetable.) Cover the vegetables with the stock and bake for about 1 hour. After an hour, check with a small knife to see if the vegetables are soft.

Sprinkle with the parsley, if using, and drizzle with more olive oil before serving.

# Stuffed tomatoes

*Punjene pome*

SERVES 4

8 large truss tomatoes

2 garlic cloves, chopped

50 ml (1¾ fl oz) extra-virgin olive oil

1 brown onion, chopped

1 eggplant (aubergine), peeled and finely diced

2 zucchini (courgettes), finely diced

2 capsicums (bell peppers), finely diced

1 tablespoon chopped basil

1 tablespoon red wine vinegar

chilli powder, for sprinkling

sea salt

freshly ground black pepper

**Like all true Mediterraneans, Croatians love the tomato. The thought of tomatoes always takes me back to the lunch table during the summer holidays when I was young. My mind goes to an old pier, from where we would dive into the sea, then I visualise myself at the table eating this dish. I can still remember how the tomatoes tasted. This recipe includes two stuffing variations.**

## Tomatoes stuffed with vegetables

Wash the tomatoes, cut off the tops and reserve. Using a teaspoon, scoop out the tomato seeds, leaving the flesh. Season the tomatoes on the inside with salt then turn them upside down until all the liquid comes out, about 15 minutes.

In a saucepan over high heat, sauté the garlic in the oil for 10 seconds. Add the onion and sauté on low heat for 10 minutes until soft. Add the remaining vegetables to the pan, season with salt and pepper and sauté for 15–20 minutes until the vegetables soften and cook through.

Transfer the vegetables to a bowl. Add the basil and vinegar, mix well and chill for a few hours in the refrigerator.

Preheat the oven to 180°C (350°F).

When the vegetable mixture is cold, sprinkle a little bit of chilli powder into the hollowed-out tomatoes, fill the tomatoes with the vegetable mixture and replace the tomato tops. Bake in the oven for 10 minutes. Serve hot or cold as an appetiser or part of a mixed appetiser platter.

8 large truss tomatoes

2 garlic cloves, chopped

50 ml (1¾ fl oz) extra-virgin olive oil

1 brown onion, chopped

500 g (1 lb 2 oz) tinned tuna

50 g (1¾ oz) capers

2 tablespoons chopped flat-leaf (Italian) parsley

1 tablespoon chopped basil

sea salt

freshly ground black pepper

•

## Tomatoes stuffed with tuna and capers

Wash the tomatoes, cut off the tops and reserve. Using a teaspoon, scoop out the tomato seeds, leaving the flesh. Season the tomatoes on the inside with salt then turn them upside down until all the liquid comes out, about 15 minutes.

In a saucepan over high heat, sauté the garlic in the oil for 10 seconds. Add the onion and sauté on low heat for 10 minutes until soft. Add the tuna and capers and sauté for 5 minutes on high heat. Remove from the heat, season with salt and pepper, add the parsley and basil and leave to cool slightly.

Preheat the oven to 180°C (350°F).

When the tuna mixture is cool, use it to fill the tomatoes then replace the tomato tops. Bake in the oven for 10 minutes. Serve hot or cold as an appetiser or part of a mixed appetiser platter.

# White bean salad

*Salata od bijelog graha*

SERVES 4

300 g (10½ oz/1½ cups)
dried cannellini (lima)
beans

5 spring onions
(scallions), sliced

4 red radishes, sliced
into rounds

2 cups crispy cos
(romaine) lettuce, sliced
into strips

50 ml (1¾ fl oz) extra-
virgin olive oil

20 ml (¾ fl oz) red
wine vinegar

1 anchovy, chopped

sea salt

freshly ground black
pepper

•

If you need a colourful salad to enhance the look of your lunch, try this recipe. You can use tinned beans – just don't tell anyone! (In Croatia, we always use dried beans and cook them from scratch.) This is a traditional salad with the addition of crispy lettuce to add texture. It can accompany fish or meat, or it makes a vibrant vegetarian appetiser.

Soak the dried beans overnight. The next day, drain the beans and transfer to a saucepan. Cover with fresh water, bring them to the boil, then cook over medium heat for 10–15 minutes, skimming off any foam that rises to the surface, until the beans are soft. Season the water at the end when the beans are soft. Turn off the heat and let the beans sit in the water for another 5 minutes. Drain off most of the water, but leave a little to keep the beans moist. Leave to cool.

Strain the cooled beans and add the spring onion, radish, lettuce, olive oil, vinegar and anchovy. Season well with salt and pepper and serve.

# Lentil, apple and pomegranate salad

*Salata od leće jabuke i nara*

SERVES 4

300 g (10½ oz) tiny
blue-green lentils

2 apples, finely diced

seeds from 1 pomegranate

1 red onion, finely diced

2 anchovies, chopped

½ bunch flat-leaf (Italian)
parsley, chopped

4 tablespoons extra-
virgin olive oil

2 tablespoons red
wine vinegar

sea salt

freshly ground black
pepper

•

In Croatia, we eat lentils frequently, adding them to soups, stews and salads. They are rich in minerals, vitamins and protein. The addition of pomegranate and apple makes this the perfect superfood salad. If you are health conscious, this is a nutritious salad that makes a great lunch or light supper.

Rinse the lentils with water to remove any dust or debris. Put them in a saucepan with 900 ml (30½ fl oz) water and bring to the boil. Cover and simmer over low heat until cooked, about 15–20 minutes.

When the lentils are tender, season them with salt and pepper – do not season the lentils before this or they will be tough. Leave to cool.

Add the apple, pomegranate, onion, anchovy and parsley to the cooled lentils and mix well to combine. Dress with the olive oil and vinegar, adjust the seasoning if needed, then serve.

# Grilled potato and spring onion salad
*Pole od krumpira s mladim lukom*

SERVES 4

1 kg (2 lb 3 oz) waxy
potatoes, such as desiree,
sebago or nicola

3 tablespoons vegetable
oil

100 ml (3½ fl oz) extra-
virgin olive oil

1 bunch spring onions
(scallions), sliced
diagonally

2 garlic cloves, crushed

3 tablespoons red
wine vinegar

sea salt

freshly ground black
pepper

•

**My father makes this dish all the time. He loves to cook potatoes in the ashes next to the open fire and use his own home-made olive oil to dress it. Wood fire adds a special smoky twist to this dish.**

Preheat a barbecue grill plate or chargrill pan to high.

Leaving the skins on, wash the potatoes and cut them in half lengthways. Put the potatoes in a bowl, sprinkle with the vegetable oil and season well with salt.

Grill the potatoes, cut side down, on the barbecue until cooked, about 10 minutes each side. When the potatoes are cooked and soft in the middle, let them cool down a little. (Alternatively, you can bake the potatoes in a 220°C/430°F oven, or wrap the cut potatoes in foil and drop them into an open fire to cook for about 20–25 minutes.)

While the potatoes are still warm, either slice them, or break them up roughly into pieces using your hands. Put them in a bowl with the olive oil, spring onion, garlic and red wine vinegar. Adjust the seasoning to taste and serve the salad warm or cold.

# Tomato and green bean salad

*Salata od rajčica i mahuna*

SERVES 4

600 g (1 lb 5 oz) tomatoes, chopped into small pieces

400 g (14 oz) green beans, cut into quarters

150 g (5½ oz) spelt

1 red onion, thinly sliced

½ cup mint leaves

50 ml (1¾ fl oz) extra-virgin olive oil

20 ml (¾ fl oz) red wine vinegar

sea salt

freshly ground black pepper

**Tomatoes always taste best from your own garden. When I was growing up in Croatia, in summer a large section of our vegie patch was reserved for tomatoes. They coloured our summer table in dazzling salads, stews, bakes and pasta sauces. Even today, now I'm living in Australia, you will still find tomato plants in the sunniest part of my backyard.**

Season the tomato well with salt and place it in a colander set over a shallow plate or bowl. Transfer to the refrigerator and chill overnight – the tomato will lose some water and the flavour will intensify.

Cook the beans in boiling seasoned water for 5 minutes, then drain and immediately refresh in ice-cold water. Drain again.

In a separate pan, cook the spelt in seasoned water for about 18 minutes. Drain and cool.

Put the beans, tomato, onion, spelt and mint in a serving bowl and mix to combine. Dress with the olive oil and vinegar, season well with salt and pepper and serve.

chapter two

# FISH AND SEAFOOD

·

•

In Croatia, we have a saying that fish swim three times: in the sea, in the olive oil and in the wine.

•

The Dalmatian coast and archipelago is a magical place. The sea is crystal clear with thousands of islands, reefs, channels and bays. Many rivers flow into the Adriatic, making it abundant with fish and shellfish species. Seafood from the Adriatic is some of the tastiest in the world – the higher salinity and nutrition from the rivers running into the Adriatic give the seafood a special flavour.

The most important thing when cooking fish and seafood is to ensure the fish is fresh. How do you do that? Do you check the expiry date? No, not really. The first sign is the eyes – they have to be clear, round and black in colour, and not white, pale or sunken. Second, the gills have to be a bright red colour (lift up the gill and have a look). Third, the fish has to smell fresh, just like the sea and not like a rubbish bin that has been sitting in the sun. Lastly, if your fish seller lets you touch the fish, the flesh should feel firm and not leave finger marks. Always try to buy local fish and buy what looks best – if you want to buy snapper but the whiting looks fresher, go with the whiting.

In Dalmatia we divide seafood into white fish (usually reef fish with white flesh, like snapper, mullet, garfish, monkfish, rockling or john dory), blue fish (oily deep-sea fish, like tuna, sardines, mackerel or swordfish), cephalopods (octopus, calamari, cuttlefish, arrow squid or squid) and shellfish. White fish is highly regarded and is usually more expensive – the bigger the fish, the higher the price.

Larger fish is usually barbecued, always with the bones, and then dressed with good olive oil, parsley and garlic. In Croatia, we have a saying that fish swim three times: in the sea, in the olive oil and in the wine. For barbecuing we use three kinds of wood – usually dry trimmings from vines, česmina (Dalmatian oak) and pine – to add to the flavour. Smaller fish is fried or used for soups and brudet (traditional fish stew). Calamari and cuttlefish are also popular, grilled, fried or made into Black risotto (page 84). Squid is usually used for bait and not for cooking. Frogs' legs are popular in Croatia, and old watermills that have now become restaurants serve this speciality.

In Dalmatian towns, the fish market is one of my go-to places during the day, to check the daily selection, buy some fish and catch up on gossip. In my town, Split, we have a beautiful old fish market. Next to the market there are mineral sulphur baths and, for this reason, this fish market is probably the only one in the world without flies. The mineral springs are one of the reasons the Roman emperor Diocletian chose to build his palace here.

# Fish soup

*Riblja juha*

**Soup is an essential part of the Croatian diet and is a must for Sunday lunch. My grandmother cooked this soup nearly every day. She used to say that it was so good it could bring people back from the dead! It is very healthy and light on the stomach, but I'm not so sure it has the powers my grandmother claimed. This is a very simple recipe. All you need is fresh fish, vegetables, olive oil, some rice and seasoning. Be sure to use white-fleshed fish for this recipe, rather than oily fish.**

Gut and scale the fish, then wash it in cold water.

Chop the vegetables and put them in a large saucepan with the fish and bay leaf. Add 1.5 litres (51 fl oz/6 cups) water and the olive oil. Season with salt and pepper. If you would like to have poached fish with a weaker soup, fill the pan with hot water, but if you would like a heartier soup, fill the pan with cold water. Bring to the boil then turn the heat to low and simmer for 40 minutes. (If the water starts to evaporate, add some more.) The olive oil will emulsify into the liquid, giving the soup a light yellow colour and a velvety texture.

Strain the soup, reserving the fish, then add the rice. Remove the fish flesh from the bones and set aside. Cook the rice until soft, about 15 minutes. Adjust the seasoning, then pour the soup into serving bowls topped with pieces of fish. Drizzle with olive oil, sprinkle with parsley and serve.

**Note:** *Instead of a whole fish, you can just use a fish head and bones. Make sure you clean the gills and blood and discard before serving.*

SERVES 4

1 kg (2 lb 3 oz) whole fish, such as flathead, rockling, snapper or eel

1 brown onion

1 garlic bulb, cut in half

2 celery stalks

1 bay leaf

100 ml (3½ fl oz) good-quality olive oil, plus extra for drizzling

50 g (1¾ oz) short-grain white rice

sea salt

freshly ground black pepper

2 tablespoons chopped flat-leaf (Italian) parsley, to serve

# Red and white baccalá

*Bakalar na bijelo i na crveno*

SERVES 4

400–500 g (14 oz–1 lb 2 oz)
baccalá

1 brown onion,
thinly sliced

½ garlic bulb, peeled
and chopped

4 tomatoes, crushed

100 ml (3½ fl oz) milk

100 ml (3½ fl oz) extra-
virgin olive oil

1 kg (2 lb 3 oz) waxy
potatoes, such as desiree,
sebago or nicola, peeled
and sliced 1 cm (½ in)
thick

½ bunch flat-leaf (Italian)
parsley, chopped

1 teaspoon honey
(optional)

**It is traditional in European Catholic countries to have baccalá while fasting during Lent. It's also usually eaten on Fridays, especially on Good Friday and Christmas Eve. It is regarded as a clean food for the soul by the Catholic clergy. There are hundreds of recipes for baccalá throughout Spain, Portugal, France, Italy and Croatia.**

**For my family, Christmas Eve is unimaginable without baccalá on the table – its smell permeates through the house announcing that a feast is about to begin.**

**Baccalá is sourced from Norway and Portugal, as there is no baccalá in the Mediterranean. My family prefer air-dried (unsalted) Norwegian cod, which is superior in quality and price. Salted Portuguese cod is also good and a lot cheaper. In Croatia, the following two recipes are the most popular. Serve it at the beginning of a meal with toasted bread.**

## Red baccalá

Soak the baccalá in cold water for 3 days, changing the water every day, then drain.

Clean the baccalá from the bones (you can leave the skin on) and cut it into small pieces, approximately 3 cm (1¼ in).

In a food processor, blend the onion, garlic and tomato until you have a smooth paste.

Put the paste, baccalá, milk, olive oil and enough water just to cover the ingredients in a saucepan over medium heat. Season well and cook for 20–30 minutes. Add the potato and a little water if necessary and cook for another 30 minutes, shaking the pot – but try not to break up the baccalá too much.

When it's a nice and creamy consistency, sprinkle with parsley and serve. I like to add a teaspoon of honey to round the flavour and give a better aroma to the baccalá.

Continued ...

# Red and white baccalá *continued* ...

SERVES 4

400–500 g (14 oz–1 lb 2 oz)
baccalá

1 kg (2 lb 3 oz) waxy
potatoes, such as desiree,
sebago or nicola, peeled
and roughly chopped

1 garlic bulb, cloves
separated and peeled

100 ml ($3\frac{1}{2}$ fl oz) milk

250 ml ($8\frac{1}{2}$ fl oz/1 cup)
extra-virgin olive oil

sea salt

freshly ground black
pepper

$\frac{1}{2}$ bunch flat-leaf
(Italian) parsley, chopped
(optional)

## White baccalá

Soak the baccalá in cold water for 3 days, changing the water every day,
then drain.

Cook the soaked baccalá in salted water until it softens and the skin starts
to break up, about 30 minutes. Take the fish out of the water (reserving the
water) and pick the meat from the skin and bones.

Cook the potato in the water in which you cooked the baccalá, until
the potato is soft and starts to break up. Strain the potato but reserve the
cooking water.

Cook the garlic in the milk over medium heat for about 10–15 minutes.
Strain and reserve the milk.

Combine the baccalá, potato and garlic in a bowl. Mash with a metal
potato masher, slowly adding the extra-virgin olive oil. Add a little of the
reserved garlic-infused milk and a little of the potato cooking water if
necessary, to work the mixture into a creamy paste. Season with salt and
pepper, add the parsley, if using, and serve.

# Marinated and pickled sardines

*Marinada od srdela i ukiseljene srdele*

For thousands of years, sardines have been a staple food of the Croatian coastal region and, in Dalmatia, we eat them frequently during the hot summer months. Marinated sardines can keep in the refrigerator for a number of weeks. They make a perfect, quick-to-prepare meal if you have unexpected guests, or are excellent served as an appetiser.

I learned this pickled sardine recipe from our neighbour in Split, when I lived there as a child. Usually, we use anchovies in this pickle recipe instead of sardines, but in Australia fresh anchovies aren't available – don't worry, sardines work just as well.

## Marinated sardines

For the marinade, combine the olive oil, vinegar, sugar, garlic, parsley, lemon zest and rosemary and bring to the boil in a saucepan.

Preheat a barbecue grill plate or chargrill pan to high.

For the sardines, scale and gut them with a small knife – cut the heads off and pull the guts out. Clean and dry them with a clean tea towel (dish towel), but don't wash them. Cover the sardines with a little oil and season with salt and pepper.

Grill the sardines on the hot barbecue until cooked, about 5 minutes each side. They should be nice and brown.

Put the grilled sardines in a stainless steel or glass dish, layering them in opposite directions. Pour the marinade over the sardines, allow the dish to cool and then refrigerate. Serve in the marinade.

SERVES 4

1 kg (2 lb 3 oz) whole fresh sardines

MARINADE

250 ml (8½ fl oz/1 cup) extra-virgin olive oil

125 ml (4 fl oz/½ cup) red wine vinegar

20 g (¾ oz) sugar

3 garlic cloves, chopped

½ bunch flat-leaf (Italian) parsley, chopped

zest of ¼ lemon

1 tablespoon rosemary

sea salt

freshly ground black pepper

SARDINES

2 kg (4 lb 6 oz) whole
fresh sardines

300 g (10½ oz) coarse sea
salt

1 litre (34 fl oz/4 cups)
white vinegar (not white
wine vinegar)

100 g (3½ oz) sugar

vegetable oil (sunflower or
cottonseed)

RED RADISH SALAD

5 red radishes, finely
diced

1 tomato, cored and
finely diced

3 spring onions
(scallions), thinly sliced

DRESSING

50 ml (1¾ fl oz) extra-
virgin olive oil

30 ml (1 fl oz) red wine
vinegar

10 ml (¼ fl oz) Varenik
(see page 35)

•

# Pickled sardines with red radish salad

For the sardines, scale and gut them with a small knife – cut the heads off and pull the guts out. Quickly wash the sardines and dry them with a clean tea towel (dish towel).

In a colander, mix the cleaned sardines with the coarse salt and leave to cure for 2 hours. Rinse the sardines and place them in a plastic or glass container.

Mix the vinegar with the sugar and pour the mixture into the container with the sardines. Make sure all the sardines are submerged in the vinegar. Leave to marinate for 24 hours.

The following day, take the sardines out of the vinegar and, using your fingers, gently butterfly them and pull the middle bone out, leaving only the tail. Arrange the sardines in layers in a glass container with an airtight lid and pour the vegetable oil over each layer of the sardines. They should be well covered in oil. Seal the container and store in the refrigerator. They will last for a long time sealed but, once opened, keep refrigerated and eat within a week.

To serve, take the sardines out of the oil, remove any excess oil and arrange them on a serving plate.

For the radish salad, mix all the ingredients together and sprinkle on top of the sardines with the dressing.

# Crab Dalmatian-style

*Grancigula na dalmatinski*

**Crabs are an extremely tasty treat. It might take time to clean the crabmeat from the shells, but it's worth it. This crab dish is usually served with a crisp green salad at the beginning of a meal.**

Wash and scrub the crabs under running water. Cook the crabs upside down in boiling salted water for about 10 minutes.

Allow the crabs to cool then remove all the meat from the legs. Carefully scrape all the meat from the head, removing the gills and intestines. Reserve the head shells, and put all the cleaned crabmeat in a bowl.

In a frying pan over medium heat, sauté the onion and garlic in the olive oil until golden brown. Add the onion and garlic to the bowl with the crabmeat.

Soak the bread in water, then squeeze out any excess and add the bread to the bowl with the crabmeat.

Break the fish fillet into small pieces and add it to the crab mixture. Add the parsley and lemon juice, season well with salt and pepper and mix together until well combined.

Grease the crab head shells with more olive oil and fill them with the crabmeat mixture.

Preheat the oven to 200°C (400°F).

Combine the breadcrumbs, cheese and a little olive oil, season with salt and pepper then cover the crabs evenly with this mixture. Put the crab shells on a baking tray and bake until the breadcrumbs and cheese become crispy and golden, about 20–25 minutes.

Combine the lettuce and radish in a bowl, dress with olive oil and vinegar and season. Serve the crabs with the salad on the side.

SERVES 4

4 crabs

1 brown onion, finely chopped

3 garlic cloves

50 ml (1¾ fl oz) extra-virgin olive oil

1 slice white bread

200 g (7 oz) pre-grilled fish, snapper or any white-fleshed fish fillet

½ bunch flat-leaf (Italian) parsley, chopped

juice of 1 lemon

2 tablespoons dry breadcrumbs

50 g (1¾ oz) paški cheese (or parmesan or cheddar), grated

sea salt

freshly ground black pepper

SALAD

200 g (7 oz) lettuce

6 red radishes

50 ml (1¾ fl oz) extra-virgin olive oil

20 ml (¾ fl oz) white wine vinegar

# Mixed small fried fish

*Frigana riba*

SERVES 4

1 kg (2 lb 3 oz) mixed
small fish, such as red
mullet, sand whiting,
smelt or bream

1 tablespoon sea salt, plus
extra for seasoning

500 ml (17 fl oz/2 cups)
milk

200 g (7 oz/1⅓ cups) plain
(all-purpose) flour

300 ml (10 fl oz)
vegetable oil

1 lemon, halved or cut
into wedges

freshly ground black
pepper

•

**My grandparents have a house on the shores of the Adriatic. They used to have a small boat that my late grandfather went out in every day to catch fish. Usually, the catch were small mixed fish that my grandmother used to fry as soon as they were brought to the kitchen. Once, my grandfather lost his fish trap. He found it two weeks later, so full of fish that he needed help to pull it out of the sea. There were two huge lobsters in the trap along with the fish. My grandmother still has one of those huge lobsters preserved on her kitchen wall to remember that lucky day. Serve these fish with a green salad or Dalmatian silverbeet (page 42).**

Clean the fish (scale and gut them), then wash them. Combine the milk and 1 tablespoon salt, then soak the fish in the milk mixture for 1 hour.

Drain the fish, then toss it in the flour, shaking off the excess.

Heat the oil in a frying pan to 190°C (375°F), or until a cube of bread turns golden in 10 seconds, and fry the fish for a couple of minutes (not putting too many fish in the pan at once) until golden.

Drain the fish on paper towel to absorb any excess oil, season well with salt and serve with the lemon wedges for squeezing.

# Black risotto

*Crni rižot*

SERVES 4

2 tablespoons
chopped garlic

100 ml (3½ fl oz) extra-
virgin olive oil

200 g (7 oz) brown
onions, chopped

1 kg (2 lb 3 oz) cuttlefish

1 tablespoon tomato paste
(concentrated purée)

100 ml (3½ fl oz)
white wine

600 ml (20½ fl oz/
2½ cups) fish stock
or water

½ tablespoon cuttlefish
ink (see method)

300 g (10½ oz) risotto rice
(arborio or carnaroli)

sea salt

freshly ground black
pepper

•

There are some dishes in Croatia, like this risotto, which we call specijaliteti, which means they are just special. You could call this the magical dish of the Adriatic, because it will enchant your taste buds.

There is a silver sac inside cuttlefish that is full of black ink (the cuttlefish releases this to defend itself when in danger), which is an essential part of this dish. You can also buy squid ink in a jar or in small plastic bags, but I recommend using fresh ink as it has a special flavour that makes this dish amazing. Also, make sure you use fresh and not frozen cuttlefish because the frozen ink sac will feel like it is full of sand instead of liquid and won't give the dish as good a flavour or colour.

In a frying pan over high heat, sauté the chopped garlic in a little olive oil for a few seconds, making sure it does not burn. Add the onion, reduce the heat to low, and sauté until golden and transparent, approximately 10–15 minutes. (It's important to sauté the garlic before the onion as this will help to release its aroma.)

Before cleaning out the inside and bones of the cuttlefish, carefully remove the silver sac of ink from the middle of the cuttlefish, making sure not to break it, and set it aside. Cut the cuttlefish into 1 cm (½ in) cubes.

Add the diced cuttlefish to the sautéed garlic and onion and season well with salt and pepper. Sauté the cuttlefish until all the liquid that has been released has evaporated and the cuttlefish starts to stick to the bottom of the pan, caramelising slightly. Add the tomato paste and cook for a few seconds, then add the white wine and cook until the liquid has almost completely evaporated. Add the fish stock or water, ½ tablespoon of the cuttlefish ink, and adjust the seasoning. Leave to simmer on low heat for 10 minutes.

Add the rice and cook for 16 minutes, stirring the risotto constantly until it is done (the rice should be cooked but still slightly firm). If the risotto is too thick, you can add some more fish stock and olive oil at the end. Add more seasoning if needed and serve immediately.

# Lobster risotto
*Rižot od jastoga*

SERVES 4

1 kg (2 lb 3 oz) whole lobster

100 ml (3½ fl oz) extra-virgin olive oil

4 garlic cloves, chopped

2 brown onions, chopped very finely (smaller than rice)

100 ml (3½ fl oz) white wine or prošek (Dalmatian fortified wine) or port

125 g (4½ oz) Dalmatian tomato sauce (see page 94)

700 ml (23½ fl oz) fish stock

300 g (10½ oz) risotto rice (arborio or carnaroli)

200 g (7 oz) cherry tomatoes, halved

sea salt

freshly ground black pepper

2 tablespoons chopped flat-leaf (Italian) parsley, to garnish

•

**The luscious and sweet flavour of lobster is captivating – absolute heaven for the taste buds. Make sure to pair this dish with a good dry white wine. My recommendation would be Croatian Pošip. Remember that a risotto is only as good as the stock you cook it with, so make sure your stock tastes great before you start cooking the rice. From the moment you start to add the stock to the rice, the risotto should take 16–18 minutes to cook.**

With a large knife, cut the lobster in half lengthways and pull the meat out of the shell.

Dice the lobster tail meat into 1 cm (½ in) cubes and set aside.

Heat half the olive oil in a large saucepan over high heat until it starts to smoke. Add the lobster shells and break them up with a mallet or other blunt object, such as a pestle, in the pan. Sauté until they become bright orange in colour and start to smell good. Add half the garlic and, after a few seconds, half the onion. Deglaze the pan with half the wine and cook for 5 minutes. Add the Dalmatian tomato sauce and fish stock, season to taste with salt and pepper, then bring to the boil. Reduce the heat to low and simmer for 15 minutes.

Blend the stock with a hand-held blender and strain through a fine-mesh sieve.

In a separate saucepan over high heat, sauté the remaining garlic in the remaining olive oil for a few seconds, then add the remaining chopped onion and sauté until soft but not brown. Add the rice and sauté until it starts to have a toasted nut aroma, about 5–8 minutes. Deglaze the pan with the remaining white wine and, once the wine evaporates, start ladling in the lobster stock gradually, approximately 1 ladleful at a time. As soon as the risotto thickens, add more stock, stirring constantly – this will make your risotto nice and creamy.

Once you have added the last ladleful of stock, add the diced lobster and halved cherry tomatoes. Adjust the seasoning if necessary and stir well for a couple of minutes. Serve immediately garnished with the parsley.

# Dalmatian fish stew

*Brudet*

SERVES 4

1.5 kg (3 lb 5 oz) fish (such as eel, monkfish, rockling, rock flathead, snapper, cod or whiting)

150 ml (5 fl oz) extra-virgin olive oil

10 garlic cloves, chopped

2 tablespoons chopped flat-leaf (Italian) parsley

juice of $\frac{1}{2}$ lemon

1 large brown onion, chopped

50 ml ($1\frac{3}{4}$ fl oz) tomato passata (puréed tomatoes)

100 ml ($3\frac{1}{2}$ fl oz) white wine

500 ml (17 fl oz/2 cups) fish stock

sea salt

freshly ground black pepper

soft polenta, to serve (optional)

**It takes a special touch to make this dish and it's usually the head of the household who prepares brudet in Croatia. You will need to use at least three different types of fish. Reef and rock fish with white flesh are the best. This dish is serious business and it takes time to master. This is a good recipe that really works – in my opinion, it works wonders. I hope you enjoy it. Dobar tek!**

Cut the whole fish, including skin and bones, into cutlets. Marinate the fish in half the olive oil, half the garlic, the parsley and lemon juice for a few hours.

In a large, heavy-based pan, or clay pot, set over high heat, sauté the remaining garlic in the remaining olive oil, adding the onion after a few seconds so the garlic doesn't burn. When the onion starts to brown slightly, add the passata and cook for 1 minute. Add the wine and cook until it loses its acidity, about 5 minutes.

Season each piece of fish well with salt and pepper. Place the fish in the pan and mix well, adding just enough fish stock to cover the fish. Boil rapidly over high heat. Do not stir, but rather shake the pan carefully to avoid breaking the fish and cook for 20 minutes. Take the brudet off the stove and serve with soft polenta, if desired.

# Baked flounder

*Pečeni iverak*

SERVES 4

4 flounder, 300–400 g
(10½–14 oz) each

1 loaf of day-old bread

150 ml (5 fl oz) extra-
virgin olive oil

1 whole lemon, plus extra
lemon wedges to serve

1 garlic clove, crushed

15 g (½ oz/½ cup) chopped
flat-leaf (Italian) parsley

sea salt

freshly ground black
pepper

**Flounder is a great fish to bake in the oven. It is much more suited to this cooking method than grilling because of its flat shape and delicate flesh. You can also braise it in a large pan with tomato or some shellfish. It's a really easy fish to eat because it doesn't contain many small bones. This recipe includes bread, which gives it a bit of crispiness and is a great companion to the sweet flavour of the flounder. You will need two roasting trays or tins to bake the four flounder. Serve with a salad or steamed vegetables.**

Wash and gut the fish. Cut around the head with a sharp knife and push your fingers under the skin to peel it off – it should come off easily in one piece. You can also peel the white skin off the bottom of the fish, but it's not essential.

Cut the crusts off the bread and cut the bread into 2 cm (¾ in) cubes. Place the bread in a food processor with all the remaining ingredients and blend into coarse crumbs. Season with salt and pepper. The mixture should taste nice and lemony.

Preheat the oven to 200°C (400°F).

Place the fish on two baking trays. Season the flounder well and spread the bread mixture evenly over each fish. Bake for about 15 minutes, or until the crust on the top is crispy. Serve with the lemon wedges for squeezing over the fish.

# Mussel pasta with Dalmatian tomato sauce

*Manistra s dagnjama i šalšom od poma*

## SERVES 4

400 ml (13½ fl oz) Dalmatian tomato sauce (see below)

1 teaspoon chopped chilli

400 g (14 oz) pasta, such as spaghetti, fettuccine or linguine

1 kg (2 lb 3 oz) mussels

sea salt

freshly ground black pepper

2 tablespoons chopped flat-leaf (Italian) parsley (optional)

## DALMATIAN TOMATO SAUCE

400 g (14 oz) large ripe tomatoes

3 garlic cloves, chopped

50 ml (1¾ fl oz) extra-virgin olive oil

1 tablespoon sugar

This is a very simple and beautiful dish. I love to prepare mussels with pasta – just make sure you buy fresh mussels. A good way to tell mussel freshness is by smelling them. They should smell like the sea and feel heavy, which means they are still alive with sea water in them. Also it's good to know where they come from, so always buy from a reputable supplier. If they are picked from dirty water or if they grow on iron (such as an old ship wreckage or iron chains) they can be full of metal and not recommended for consumption.

The tomato sauce recipe here can be used as a base for more complex sauces, since it doesn't have any additional flavours. You can add olives, capers, mushrooms, some ham or prosciutto, and rosemary or basil. If you don't have fresh tomatoes you can use tinned. In Croatia, we serve this sauce with poached meat or just as a plain pasta sauce. If you don't want to make the tomato sauce you can just use passata or crushed tomatoes, in which case allow just 15 minutes for cooking the sauce on low heat.

For the tomato sauce, bring some salted water to the boil in a large saucepan. Score the tomatoes at the base with a knife and blanch them for a couple of minutes. Peel the skin off the tomatoes and discard. Cut the tomatoes into 1 cm (½ in) cubes.

In another saucepan over high heat, cook the garlic in the olive oil for a few seconds, making sure it doesn't start to colour. Add the tomato and chilli and season with salt and pepper. Reduce the heat to low and cook for about 1 hour. It's very important to make sure the sauce is cooked on low heat, never going above a gentle simmer. If the sauce is cooked on too high a temperature, it will change the flavour and taste a bit dull. Adjust the seasoning and add the sugar if the tomatoes taste too acidic.

Cook the pasta in salted boiling water until al dente. Drain.

When the tomato sauce is cooked, add the mussels and cook until they just open. Add your cooked pasta, sprinkle with parsley if using, check the seasoning and serve. (Remember the mussels will be salty, so you don't need to add too much salt.)

# Pasta with anchovies

*Manistra sa srdelama*

**This is a very simple and great pasta dish if you love anchovies. I have added some almonds to the recipe, and I hope it won't offend any Croatians. Traditionally, pasta similar to spaghetti was made at home in a brass press. I don't think many people still make it at home, since buying spaghetti from the supermarket is a lot less time-consuming.**

Cook the pasta in a large saucepan of boiling salted water until al dente.

Sauté the garlic in the olive oil in a large frying pan over high heat for a few seconds until the garlic just starts to cook, but not colour. Add the anchovies, almonds, onion and chilli. Sauté over low heat until the onion is translucent and the anchovies break up. Add the breadcrumbs and sauté for 1 minute, then add the capers and parsley. Add the cooked, drained pasta, mix well, season and serve.

SERVES 4

300 g (10½ oz) spaghetti or any long thin pasta

3 garlic cloves, crushed

100 ml (3½ fl oz) extra-virgin olive oil

10 anchovies, chopped

10 almonds, chopped

½ brown onion, finely diced

1 red chilli

3 tablespoons dry breadcrumbs

1 tablespoon capers

2 tablespoons chopped flat-leaf (Italian) parsley

sea salt

freshly ground black pepper

# Cuttlefish and broad bean stew

*Brudet od sipe s bobom*

SERVES 4

1 kg (2 lb 3 oz) fresh
cuttlefish

4 garlic cloves, crushed

100 ml (3½ fl oz) extra-
virgin olive oil

2 brown onions, chopped

1 tablespoon tomato paste
(concentrated purée)

100 ml (3½ fl oz)
white wine

500 ml (17 fl oz/2 cups)
fish stock

200 g (7 oz) fresh broad
(fava) beans, podded

sea salt

freshly ground black
pepper

polenta or crusty bread,
to serve

•

**My father cooks this dish over an open fire in a heavy, cast-iron pot. Here, in Australia, he has a wood-fired oven, which in Dalmatia we call a komin. When you cook food over an open fire it adds a special smoky flavour. The combination of freshly baked bread from the wood-fired oven and this cuttlefish stew is sensational. However, you can cook this dish on the stove and it will still taste great.**

Before cleaning out the inside and bones of the cuttlefish, carefully remove the silver sac of ink from the middle of the cuttlefish, making sure not to break it. Cut the cuttlefish into 3 cm (1¼ in) cubes.

In a saucepan over low heat, sauté the garlic in the olive oil for a few seconds, making sure it does not burn. Add the onion and sauté over low heat until golden and transparent, about 10–15 minutes – note that the onion will release water and stop the garlic from burning. (It's important to sauté the garlic before the onion as this will release its flavour better.) Add the tomato paste and sauté for a few minutes to remove the acidity, then add the wine and cook until it has almost completely evaporated.

Add the diced cuttlefish to the pan and season well. Sauté for 5 minutes, add the fish stock and cuttlefish ink, then bring to the boil over medium–high heat. Reduce the heat to low and simmer for 10–15 minutes.

Peel the outer skin from the broad beans and add the beans to the stew. Cook for another 5 minutes and serve with polenta or crusty bread.

# Stuffed calamari

*Punjene lignje*

SERVES 4

1 kg (2 lb 3 oz) calamari

100 g (3½ oz) silverbeet (Swiss chard), chopped

100 ml (3½ fl oz) extra-virgin olive oil

2 tablespoons chopped garlic

50 g (1¾ oz/½ cup) dry breadcrumbs

1 kg (2 lb 3 oz) waxy potatoes, such as desiree, sebago or nicola, sliced 1 cm (½ in) thick

100 ml (3½ fl oz) white wine

2 tablespoons chopped flat-leaf (Italian) parsley, to garnish (optional)

sea salt

freshly ground black pepper

lemon wedges, to serve

•

**Calamari are a delicacy in Croatia and this is one of the most popular dishes. For this recipe it's very important to buy calamari and not squid or arrow squid, so you need to learn how to tell them apart, otherwise you will have a very tough and chewy meal. Calamari are tender and sweet and tangy in flavour – and they are more expensive. I find this dish very easy to make, but you have to be careful not to overcook the calamari. Cook the potatoes as per the recipe, or separately, as a side dish, and serve with a good white wine and a green salad.**

Clean the calamari by taking out all the intestines, the head and the tentacles. Do not remove the skin as it's full of flavour and will give the potatoes a nice red colour.

For the filling, cut the tentacles into 5 mm (¼ in) pieces. Wash and chop the silverbeet into roughly the same-sized pieces.

Put half the olive oil in a frying pan over medium heat and sauté the garlic for a few seconds, making sure it doesn't change colour. Add the calamari tentacles and silverbeet, season well with salt and pepper and cook for a minute or two. Sprinkle over the breadcrumbs and take the pan off the heat. Let the mixture cool to room temperature.

Preheat the oven to 220°C (430°F).

Stuff the calamari with the filling and close them with a toothpick or wooden skewer.

Add the sliced potatoes to a baking dish, season well and coat them with almost all the remaining olive oil. Lay the calamari on top of the potatoes. Drizzle with white wine and a little olive oil, season and cover with aluminium foil. Bake for 10 minutes, take the foil off, remove the calamari and continue to cook the potatoes for another 25–30 minutes until cooked.

Before serving, return the calamari to the baking dish with the potatoes and cook for another 10 minutes until golden brown. Sprinkle with parsley, if using, and serve hot with the lemon wedges on the side.

# Octopus salad
*Salata od hobotnice*

SERVES 4

1 kg (2 lb 3 oz) octopus

200 g (7 oz) waxy
potatoes, such as desiree,
sebago or nicola

2 bay leaves

10 peppercorns

80 ml (2½ fl oz/⅓ cup)
extra-virgin olive oil

40 ml (1¼ fl oz) red wine
vinegar

½ red onion, finely
chopped

200 g (7 oz) cherry
tomatoes, halved

2 small Lebanese (short)
cucumbers, sliced

2 garlic cloves, chopped

2 tablespoons chopped
flat-leaf (Italian) parsley

sea salt

freshly ground black
pepper

**This is one of the most popular dishes served in restaurants and konobe (traditional Croatian eateries) along the Adriatic coast. It's the perfect light and fresh start to a meal, especially on a warm summer day. There are hundreds of variations of this dish and every family treasures their own special recipe. It is fairly easy to prepare and, when you become confident in making it, you can add your own personal touch – adding some capers, salad leaves or even olives. But, whatever you do, don't put fruit in your octopus salad as this might cause you to lose your Croatian friends!**

First, you need to tenderise the octopus. In Australia, fishmongers can do this for you by spinning the octopus in an oyster-cleaning machine. If you plan to tenderise it yourself, freeze the octopus for 2–3 days, then defrost it completely and beat the octopus all over with a mallet or a rolling pin to break down the muscles.

Cook the potatoes in their skins in boiling salted water until soft. When they are cool enough to handle, peel them and cut into 1 cm (½ in) thick slices.

Bring 2 litres (68 fl oz/8 cups) water, the bay leaves and peppercorns to the boil (do not season the water with salt). Put the octopus in the boiling water and cook for 12 minutes. Strain the octopus and let it cool for 5 minutes.

Remove the octopus skin and cut the tentacles into 5 mm (¼ in) slices. Transfer to a serving dish. While the octopus is still warm, add the olive oil, vinegar, potato, onion, tomato, cucumber, garlic, parsley and season with salt and pepper to taste. Mix well and serve.

# Eel and frogs' leg stew

*Neretvanski brudet*

SERVES 6

100 ml (3½ fl oz) extra-
virgin olive oil

3 bay leaves

3 small red hot chillies,
chopped

2 brown onions, finely
chopped

3 tablespoons tomato
passata (puréed tomatoes)

1 kg (2 lb 3 oz) eel,
cleaned and cut into
3–4 cm (1¼–1½ in) pieces

18 frogs' legs or 9 chicken
drumsticks

50 ml (1¾ fl oz) white
wine vinegar

sea salt

freshly ground black
pepper

•

**At the delta of the river Neretva is the biggest orchard in Croatia, known as 'Croatian California'. It was once the home of fierce pirates who ruled the Adriatic Sea in the 9th century, but now it is a peaceful place full of citrus and vegetable farms. It is also home to many eels and frogs. This is a very traditional and special dish of that region. Usually, this dish is cooked in a heavy-based pot, but you can use a standard saucepan – just be sure to shake it constantly so the meat doesn't stick to the bottom of the pan and burn. Since frogs' legs are banned in some countries, you can use chicken drumsticks instead.**

Put the olive oil, bay leaves, chilli and onion in a saucepan over medium heat and sauté until the onion is a pale golden colour, about 10–15 minutes.

Add the passata to the pan and sauté for a couple of minutes. Season the eel well and add it to the pan (if you are using chicken, add it now). Add 600 ml (20½ fl oz) water and cook for 25–30 minutes. Make sure you don't stir it as this will break up the eel; just gently shake the pan every couple of minutes.

Add the frogs' legs and vinegar and boil for a few minutes, or until the legs are tender. Serve hot.

# Monkfish baked with tomato and beans

*Grdobina s fažolom*

SERVES 4

800 g (1 lb 12 oz) monkfish fillets

100 ml (3½ fl oz) extra-virgin olive oil

2 tablespoons chopped garlic

50 ml (1¾ fl oz) white wine

250 ml (8½ fl oz/1 cup) Dalmatian tomato sauce (see page 94)

100 ml (3½ fl oz) fish stock

300 g (10½ oz) cooked white beans, such as cannellini (lima) beans (see White bean salad, page 58, for cooking instructions)

sea salt

freshly ground black pepper

**Monkfish has a very sweet and delicate flavour and is a great fish for braises and soups. For some reason monkfish is inexpensive here in Australia, while in Europe the opposite is true. Fishermen in Croatia love to cook this fish. It was one of the first fish that I ever caught – I remember mornings spent on a gajeta (a traditional Croatian wooden fishing boat) on the calm Adriatic and the feelings of joy and pride when we pulled the monkfish out of the sea and into the boat. If you buy a whole fish, use the head to make soup or the stock for this dish.**

Wash and dry the monkfish fillets. Heat the olive oil in a large, non-stick frying pan over high heat until nearly smoking. Add the monkfish fillets. Season the fish well with salt and pepper and sear on both sides for a minute, turning them over gently with a spatula, until golden brown. Add the garlic to the pan and cook for a few seconds. Add the white wine and cook until the wine has nearly evaporated.

Preheat the oven to 220°C (430°F).

Transfer the fish to a clay pot or ovenproof baking dish. Add the tomato sauce, fish stock and cooked beans. Mix gently and adjust the seasoning. Bake in the oven for 10 minutes then serve.

# Scampi in garlic, white wine and tomato

*Škampi na buzaru*

SERVES 4

100 ml (3½ fl oz) extra-
virgin olive oil

1 kg (2 lb 3 oz) scampi
(langoustine)

4 garlic cloves, chopped

250 ml (8½ fl oz/1 cup)
white wine

125 ml (4 fl oz/½ cup)
tomato passata
(puréed tomatoes)

1 tablespoon dry
breadcrumbs

2 tablespoons chopped
flat-leaf (Italian) parsley

sea salt

freshly ground black
pepper

crusty bread, to serve

finger bowls of water with
lemon juice

This is another of the most loved dishes in Croatia. It is a typical fisherman's recipe – simple but delicious. If I have a special dinner party guest who I want to impress, škampi na buzaru is definitely on the menu. Once you try this dish, you'll realise what all the fuss is about.

Scampi from the Adriatic Sea are of exceptional quality. Don't confuse scampi with prawns (shrimp) – they are a world apart. Scampi have an exceptionally delicate, sweet flavour. There is a whole culture around eating scampi. Use your fingers to dismantle them from the shell and then take your time eating them, as they are so full of flavour and every single bit is delicious. Soak up the juices from the scampi with crusty bread.

Heat the olive oil in a saucepan over high heat, being careful not to let it start smoking. Add the scampi and sauté them on both sides for a couple of minutes. Add the garlic and cook for few seconds (be careful not to brown the garlic because this will make the dish taste bitter). Add the white wine, passata, breadcrumbs and season with salt and pepper. Cover the pan with a lid and cook for another 15 minutes, shaking the pan frequently so the scampi don't stick to the bottom and burn. If the sauce is too thick add a touch of water.

Sprinkle with the parsley and serve with the crusty bread. Provide finger bowls for your diners – this one can get messy!

# Split-style tuna
*Tunjevina na splitski*

SERVES 4

1 kg (2 lb 3 oz) tuna
steaks
olive oil, for drizzling
sea salt
freshly ground black
pepper

RED WINE AND
ONION SAUCE

2 brown onions,
thinly sliced
100 ml (3½ fl oz) extra-
virgin olive oil
4 garlic cloves, crushed
500 ml (17 fl oz/2 cups)
good red wine
50 ml (1¾ fl oz) Varenik
(see page 35) or vincotto
50 g (1¾ oz) sultanas
(golden raisins)

POTATO SALAD

3 whole waxy potatoes,
such as desiree, sebago or
nicola
½ onion, very thinly sliced
100 ml (3½ fl oz) extra-
virgin olive oil
30 ml (1 fl oz) white
wine vinegar

**This is my modern variation of a very old dish. The original recipe calls to cook the tuna in red wine for 45 minutes. I really love my tuna cooked rare, so I prepare the sauce separately and serve it with rare tuna and potato salad. Tuna is such a good match with red wine and onions, and that's what makes this dish so delicious.**

Cut the tuna into 2–3 cm (¾–1¼ in) thick slices – you should get five to six slices.

For the sauce, sauté the onion in the olive oil for 10–15 minutes on low heat until soft and translucent. Add the garlic and sauté for 5 seconds, then add the wine, varenik and sultanas and boil rapidly until the sauce thickens and has reduced by two-thirds.

For the potato salad, cook the potatoes in their skins in boiling salted water until soft. Leave them to cool for approximately 10 minutes. While still warm, peel the skins off and cut them into 1 cm (½ in) thick slices. Add the spring onion, olive oil, white wine vinegar and season well.

Preheat a barbecue grill plate or chargrill pan to high.

Grill the tuna quickly on the barbecue, for 2 minutes on each side, just to get nice char marks on the outside of the fish, leaving it raw in the middle.

Serve the tuna on the potato salad and garnish with the red wine and onion sauce. Drizzle with olive oil and serve.

chapter three

# MEAT

.

# Game is prepared with special care in Dalmatia, as it's not every day that your table is visited by nice pheasant, hare, boar or deer.

Many things have changed in Croatia since I was a child. Today, meat is bought in large supermarkets already sliced or cut into pieces and packed in plastic, and there aren't as many small butcher's shops. When I lived there, I used to buy meat for my grandmother at the local butcher – my grandmother had a problem with her legs and couldn't go out any more. She would say, 'Tell him it is for Tomica (her name) and watch he doesn't cheat on the scales'. I would tell the butcher the part of the meat my grandmother wanted and he would pull down a large piece of meat from a hook, cut it up in front of me with a huge cleaver, weigh it and wrap it in thick white paper. My grandmother would then use it to make a great soup and the meat would be served poached with tomato sauce, sautéed potatoes and salad (see page 140). Sometimes she would make a delicious beef ragu with potato dumplings. Because of those dumplings I loved to go and buy the meat for my grandmother!

Veal, beef and pork are the most popular meats and cooked in many different ways. In Dalmatia we produce some of the world's best pršut. This Dalmatian version of prosciutto is salted then smoked for a few days, which makes it distinct from its Italian and Spanish counterparts, which aren't smoked. The town of Drniš in the Dalmatian hinterland is famous for the best prosciutto – as well as the tallest people in Europe.

Many people in Croatia opposed the country joining the European Union as the EU has strict laws about livestock. Therefore, there is no more home-made pršut (prosciutto) or other smallgoods. Disaster! Most people still make these things at home, but please don't tell the EU.

Game is prepared with special care in Dalmatia, as it's not every day that your table is visited by nice pheasant, hare, boar or deer. Usually game is marinated in good red wine and vinegar overnight to tenderise it, and then cooked into rich stews and ragus. These dishes are served with potato dumplings, hand-made pastas or polenta.

# Bean and barley soup

*Juha od orza i fažola*

SERVES 6

2 garlic cloves

1 onion, chopped

1 carrot, diced or grated

1 celery stalk, chopped

2 floury potatoes, such as coliban or king edward, chopped

1 bay leaf

100 g (3½ oz) pancetta, cut into pieces, or 1 smoked ham hock

2 litres (68 fl oz/8 cups) chicken or vegetable stock

200 g (7 oz/1 cup) borlotti (cranberry) beans, soaked in water overnight then drained

200 g (7 oz) barley

1 litre (34 fl oz/4 cups) milk

1 tablespoon extra-virgin olive oil

1 tablespoon red wine vinegar

sea salt

freshly ground black pepper

2 tablespoons chopped flat-leaf (Italian) parsley, to garnish

**This is a lovely, hearty soup that is a meal in itself, best eaten on cold winter days. It's better to eat this soup a few hours after making it, or even the next day, so that all the flavours have time to develop. Barley is an ancient grain with plenty of health benefits. It can be used in salads, in soups like this or thick, rich stews.**

Place all the vegetables, the bay leaf and the pancetta or ham hock in a large saucepan over high heat and cover with the stock. Bring to the boil and simmer for 30 minutes. Add the soaked beans and simmer for another 20–30 minutes. Do not season the soup until the beans are soft.

Take around one-third of the beans and soup out of the pan and process in a blender. Return the purée to the pan (this will thicken the soup), then add the barley and milk. Season with salt and pepper and simmer for another 20 minutes until the barley is cooked through. Right at the end, add the olive oil and vinegar, garnish with parsley, then serve.

# Dubrovnik soup

## *Dubrovačka maneštra*

SERVES 6

300 g (10½ oz) smoked pork ribs or a hock

150 g (5½ oz) sheep jerky (if you can't find this, use extra smoked pork)

2 pork sausages (chorizo are good)

5 garlic cloves

100 g (3½ oz) pancetta

2 tablespoons extra-virgin olive oil

200 g (7 oz) floury potatoes, such as coliban or king edward, peeled and cut into 1.5 cm (½ in) pieces

400 g (14 oz) brussels sprouts, halved

100 g (3½ oz) zucchini (courgettes), cut into 2 cm (¾ in) dice

100 g (3½ oz) green beans, cut into 3 cm (1¼ in) pieces

sea salt

freshly ground black pepper

flat-leaf (Italian) parsley, to garnish (optional)

**Here's a traditional recipe from one of the most beautiful places in the world. This soup is as rich in flavour as Dubrovnik is in culture and history. It's a very hearty soup, which I would serve during long, cold winter nights.**

Put the pork ribs or hock, sheep jerky and sausages in a saucepan with 2.5 litres (85 fl oz/10 cups) cold water. Season with salt and pepper and cook over high heat for 40 minutes, until the meat is cooked. Take the pork, jerky and sausages out of the water and let them cool for a few minutes. Cut the pork and jerky into small pieces, discarding the bones, and slice the sausage. Reserve the cooking water in the pan. Turn off the heat.

Chop the garlic and pancetta finely or mince (grind) in a food processor, then mix with the olive oil.

Put the potato in the pan of reserved cooking water, along with the garlic and pancetta mixture. Cook for 10 minutes over high heat, then add the remaining vegetables and return the cut meats to the pan. Cook for a further 10 minutes, then serve hot sprinkled with the parsley, if using.

# Cabbage sausages

*Kaštelanski kulen*

SERVES 4

400 g (14 oz) green cabbage, finely chopped

1 brown onion, chopped into small dice

500 g (1 lb 2 oz) short-grain white rice

80 g (2¾ oz) sultanas (golden raisins)

grated zest of 1 lemon

1 whole nutmeg, freshly grated

500 ml (17 fl oz/2 cups) vegetable stock

1 m (3 ft) length of thick pork sausage casing

butcher's twine

sea salt

freshly ground black pepper

**These unusual sausages are truly delicious and relatively easy to make. After boiling, they keep well in the refrigerator for a few days and can then be barbecued, pan-fried or oven-baked. In Dalmatia there are many different versions of this recipe, but kaštelanski kulen is one of the most well-known versions. Enjoy – I know you will!**

In a large bowl mix the cabbage with the onion, rice, sultanas, lemon zest, nutmeg and vegetable stock. Season well with salt and pepper. Set aside for 1 hour.

Wash the pork sausage casing well, but do not remove the fat. Gently start to fill it with the cabbage mixture, using your hands. Make 30 cm (12 in) long sausages, tying them well with butcher's twine. Leave a space of four fingers at the end of each sausage empty, otherwise when the rice starts to cook it will expand and break the casing.

Prick the sausages with a toothpick or sewing needle and cook in salted water over low heat for about an hour. To finish, you can later grill the sausages on the barbecue, pan-fry or bake in the oven for about 10–15 minutes at 200°C (400°F).

# Rabbit the Dalmatian way

*Zec na dalmatinski*

SERVES 4

1 rabbit (approximately
2–3 kg/4 lb 6 oz–
6 lb 10 oz)

200 ml (7 fl oz) vinegar

5 garlic cloves, sliced
lengthways

100 g (3½ oz) pancetta,
sliced

100 ml (3½ fl oz) extra-
virgin olive oil

200 ml (7 fl oz)
white wine or prošek
(Dalmatian fortified
wine) or port

sea salt

freshly ground black
pepper

MAKARUNI

1 kg (2 lb 3 oz/
6⅔ cups) plain (all-
purpose) flour

1 egg

1 egg yolk

100 g (3½ oz) unsalted
butter, softened

50 ml (1¾ fl oz) vegetable
oil

1 teaspoon salt

150–200 ml (5–7 fl oz)
warm water

I have countless childhood memories of rabbits and pheasants hanging in our konoba (the basement where food and wine were stored) and of my uncle cleaning his rifle after going hunting, then putting it back in place over the kitchen door until next time. I can remember my aunt and grandmother rolling makaruni na iglu (pasta rolled with a knitting needle), which goes extremely well with rabbit. I have given the recipe below, but you can use other pasta if you like.

Game is always served on special occasions and is a very delicate food – it takes lots of careful preparation to get it just right. For this dish you can use wild or farmed rabbit. If you are buying wild rabbit, make sure it is not too large as older rabbits are tough and have less flavour. You will need to leave wild rabbit to marinate for an extra day since the muscles are much tougher with very little fat. On the other hand, farmed rabbits are bred for eating and are sold at the best time for consumption.

Cut the rabbit into portion-sized pieces (about 8 cm/3¼ in) and leave to marinate overnight in the vinegar and 500 ml (17 fl oz/2 cups) water, to allow the meat to soften.

The next day, take the rabbit out of the marinade, wash it well with water then pat it dry with a clean tea towel (dish towel).

For the makaruni, mix the flour with the egg, egg yolk, softened butter, oil and salt in a bowl. Gradually add the warm water and knead the mixture into a smooth dough. Let the dough rest for 30 minutes in the refrigerator. Cut the dough into small pieces, approximately the size of a broad (fava) bean or the tip of your finger. Roll them out with a bamboo stick or knitting needle into tubes. When rolled, they should be about 5–8 cm (2–3¼ in) in length.

Continued ...

# Rabbit the Dalmatian way *continued ...*

## SAUCE

1 carrot, finely diced

1 brown onion, finely diced

100 ml ($3\frac{1}{2}$ fl oz) extra-virgin olive oil

2 bay leaves

1 rosemary sprig

1 sage sprig

$\frac{1}{2}$ bunch flat-leaf (Italian) parsley, chopped

juice of 2 lemons

500 ml (17 fl oz/2 cups) chicken stock

3 tablespoons sugar

Preheat the oven to 200°C (400°F). Pierce the rabbit and place the sliced garlic in the slits. Season the rabbit with salt and pepper and coat it with slices of pancetta. Lay the meat in a baking dish, pour the olive oil and white wine or prošek over it and roast for 30 minutes.

While the rabbit is roasting, prepare the sauce. Sauté the carrot and onion in the olive oil in a frying pan over high heat for approximately 10 minutes. Add the bay leaves, rosemary, sage, pepper, parsley, lemon juice, chicken stock and sugar. Season to taste with salt and pepper. Bring to the boil then pour the sauce over the rabbit. Reduce the heat to 180°C (350°F) and roast for another hour.

Serve the rabbit with the pasta.

# Poached chicken with olives

*Kokoš s maslinama*

SERVES 4

1 whole chicken
2 bay leaves
20 peppercorns
2 carrots
1 brown onion
2 celery stalks
sea salt
freshly ground black
pepper

SALSA

160 ml (5½ fl oz) extra-
virgin olive oil
1 onion
1 tablespoon chopped
flat-leaf (Italian) parsley
2 anchovies, chopped
8 olives, pitted and
roughly chopped
3 tablespoons red
wine vinegar
zest of 1 lemon

**This traditional Dalmatian dish is great to prepare in advance and can be refrigerated for a few days before eating. It's a hearty meal but is a delight to eat all year round, regardless of the season. After making this recipe, you'll be left with a light chicken stock, which you can use as the base for a lovely soup. It's best to prepare this dish in the morning if you're planning to serve it for dinner. Serve it cold with some boiled potatoes and a leafy green salad.**

For the salsa, put the olive oil in a bowl and grate the onion on top. Add the remaining salsa ingredients, season well with salt and pepper and mix well to combine. Set aside.

In a large stockpot, bring 5 litres (170 fl oz/20 cups) water to the boil and season with salt.

Stuff the chicken with the bay leaves and peppercorns. Add the remaining ingredients to the stockpot, making sure the chicken stays submerged 3 cm (1¼ in) under the water. Simmer on medium heat for about 40–50 minutes, until the chicken is cooked through.

Take the chicken out of what has now become stock (reserving the stock for soup) and transfer the chicken to a serving dish. While still warm, cut the chicken into pieces and cover it with the salsa, turning the meat over gently to cover all sides but being careful not to break it up. Let the meat cool, then serve.

# Stuffed spatchcock

*Punjeni pilići*

**This is a great dish for Sunday lunch. Traditionally in Croatia on Sunday we serve a good bone broth soup followed by a roast. Normally this dish is served with roast vegetables and a hand-cut pasta called rezanci. The pasta is cooked in water then drained and put in the roasting tray with the spatchcock to soak up all the roasting juices. Make sure you leave some room for dessert!**

SERVES 4

4 spatchcock (poussin) (each approximately 500 g/1 lb 2 oz)

50 g (1¾ oz) butter, melted

1 red capsicum (bell pepper), thickly sliced

5 shallots, halved

8 waxy potatoes, such as desiree, sebago or nicola, halved

100 g (3½ oz) lard, melted and kept hot

STUFFING

1 brown onion, finely chopped

50 ml (1¾ fl oz) extra-virgin olive oil

1 garlic clove, crushed

3 slices of bread

250 ml (8½ fl oz/1 cup) milk

200 g (7 oz) minced (ground) veal (from the shoulder or neck)

100 g (3½ oz) chicken livers

50 g (1¾ oz) smoked bacon

1 egg, beaten

1 rosemary sprig, chopped

To make the stuffing, heat the olive oil in a frying pan over high heat and sauté the onion until golden brown. When it's almost done, add the garlic and sauté for another couple of minutes. Leave the onion and garlic to cool.

Soak the bread in the milk then squeeze most of the milk out of the bread and set aside.

In a mincer (grinder), mince the veal, chicken livers, smoked bacon and softened bread. If you don't have a mincer you could chop it all finely with a knife.

Put the minced meat in a bowl, add the cooled onion and garlic mixture, the egg and rosemary. Season well with salt and pepper.

For this dish you can debone the spatchcock or just fill the cavity without deboning. If you are deboning the spatchcock, cut the spines out using kitchen scissors. With a boning knife, remove all the bones except the bones in the legs and wings.

Brush the inside of the spatchcock with the butter and season well. Stuff the spatchcock with the filling and close with a skewer.

If you are not deboning the spatchcock, just place the stuffing inside and close the bird with a skewer or toothpick.

Preheat the oven to 190°C (375°F).

Put the spatchcock in a greased roasting tin. Arrange the vegetables around the birds. Pour the hot lard over the spatchcock and vegetables and bake for 30 minutes, basting with the pan juices from the bottom of the tin every 5–10 minutes. Serve hot.

# Duck with sauerkraut

*Patka sa zeljem*

SERVES 4

1 kg (2 lb 3 oz) duck (with the bones), cut into 8 cm (3¼ in) pieces, or cook the duck whole

2 teaspoons paprika (hot or mild)

¼ teaspoon freshly grated nutmeg

50 ml (1¾ fl oz) extra-virgin olive oil

100 g (3½ oz) pancetta, finely diced

4 garlic cloves, chopped

500 g (1 lb 2 oz) Sauerkraut (page 52)

2 bay leaves

1 cinnamon stick

500 ml (17 fl oz/2 cups) vegetable stock

sea salt

freshly ground black pepper

**This is a dish to satisfy your heart and soul during the colder months. The rich flavour of the duck complements the sauerkraut perfectly. It's not difficult to make and it can keep in the refrigerator for a week. This kind of dish always tastes better the next day, so I recommend cooking it the day before. You can serve it with mashed potato or just some good crusty bread.**

Season the duck with salt, paprika and nutmeg. Heat the olive oil in an cast-iron pan or clay pot over high heat.

Add the duck to the pan and sear until nice and golden brown. Remove the duck from the pan and transfer to a plate. Add the pancetta and sauté until golden brown. Add the garlic and sauté for a couple of seconds then add the sauerkraut. Sauté on low heat for 10–15 minutes until the sauerkraut becomes a nice golden colour.

Return the duck to the dish with the bay leaves, cinnamon stick and vegetable stock. Braise on low heat, or bake in the oven at 190°C (375°F), for 1 hour. If necessary, add more vegetable stock to loosen the mixture a little. Serve straight from the pan.

# Quail Levant

*Prepelica na levantski*

SERVES 4

4 quails, cleaned

8 slices pancetta

butcher's twine

100 g (3½ oz) unsalted butter, plus extra for pan-frying the bread

4 preserved vine leaves

100 ml (3½ fl oz) chicken or vegetable stock

100 ml (3½ fl oz) white wine

200 g (7 oz) yoghurt

4 slices bread

sea salt

freshly ground black pepper

STUFFING

50 ml (1¾ fl oz) extra-virgin olive oil

½ brown onion, chopped

150 g (5½ oz) minced (ground) beef or pork

50 g (1¾ oz) sultanas (golden raisins)

1 slice of bread soaked in milk

zest of ½ lemon

1 tablespoon chopped flat-leaf (Italian) parsley

**As its name suggests, this recipe comes from the Levant in the eastern Mediterranean region. Maybe a long time ago, someone such as the Croatian-born merchant Marco Polo ate this dish somewhere in Constantinople or Alexandria, loved it and decided to make it when he returned home. Many centuries have passed since then, but this dish has remained in our culture. Its name is a reminder of its origins.**

To make the stuffing, heat the olive oil in a frying pan over high heat and sauté the onion for a couple of minutes. Set the onion aside to cool.

Put the minced meat, sultanas, bread soaked in milk (squeeze the excess milk out of the bread first), lemon zest, parsley and onion in a bowl and season well with salt and pepper. Mix well until all the ingredients are incorporated, about 5 minutes.

Stuff the quails with the filling and cover them with pancetta slices. Tie the quails with butcher's twine and sauté them in the butter in a saucepan over high heat until golden brown, about 2 minutes each side. Remove the quails from the pan, untie the twine and remove the pancetta. Wrap the quails in the vine leaves and return to the same saucepan. Pour over the chicken stock and white wine, cover with a lid, and cook over medium heat for about 15–20 minutes.

The quails are cooked if the juices run clear when the meat is pierced in the thickest part of the leg. Take them out of the pan. If there is too much liquid left in the pan, boil rapidly until the liquid has almost completely reduced, then stir in the yoghurt to make the sauce.

In a separate frying pan set over high heat, fry the slices of bread in a little butter or vegetable oil until golden brown. Place the bread on a serving plate, top with the quail and pour over the yoghurt sauce. Serve.

# Partridge risotto

*Tingulet od jarebice*

SERVES 4

2 partridges, each 500 g
(1 lb 2 oz)

100 ml ($3\frac{1}{2}$ fl oz) extra-
virgin olive oil

2 garlic cloves, chopped

1 brown onion,
finely chopped

185 g ($6\frac{1}{2}$ oz/1 cup) risotto
rice (arborio or carnaroli)

100 ml ($3\frac{1}{2}$ fl oz) red wine

100 g ($3\frac{1}{2}$ oz) prunes

600 ml ($20\frac{1}{2}$ fl oz) hot
chicken stock

50 g ($1\frac{3}{4}$ oz/$\frac{1}{2}$ cup)
grated parmesan

50 g ($1\frac{3}{4}$ oz) butter

sea salt

freshly ground black
pepper

2 tablespoons chopped
flat-leaf (Italian) parsley
(optional)

**This is a great risotto. The tangy, game flavour of partridge and the sweetness of the prunes give this dish a special balance. Tingulet, as we call it, can be made with any kind of feathered game. If you can't find game birds, you can make it with duck or chicken, which will work just as well.**

Cut the partridges into 3 cm (1¼ in) pieces with kitchen scissors then season well with salt and pepper.

In a heavy-based saucepan over high heat, cook the partridge in the olive oil until golden brown on both sides. Remove the partridge from the pan, add the garlic and sauté it for just a few seconds – don't let it colour. Add the onion (this will stop the garlic from burning) and sauté on medium–low heat until translucent. Add the rice and sauté for a couple of minutes, until it has a nice nutty aroma. Add the wine and stir until it is completely absorbed into the rice.

Return the partridge to the pan along with the prunes. Add enough hot chicken stock to just cover the rice and partridge and stir gently. Keep adding the stock, after each ladleful has been absorbed, until the rice is cooked, about 16 minutes. Finally, adjust the seasoning and add the parmesan and butter. Stir until you have a creamy consistency, garnish with the parsley, if using, and serve.

# Poached meat

*Lešo meso*

SERVES 4

1 kg (2 lb 3 oz) mixed meat (chicken wings, beef neck and lamb cutlets)

2 brown onions, with the skin still on, cut into quarters

2 carrots

2 celery stalks

2 tomatoes, halved

½ celeriac, peeled

4 garlic cloves

50 ml (1¾ fl oz) extra-virgin olive oil

2 tablespoons chopped flat-leaf (Italian) parsley

1 teaspoon peppercorns

sea salt

Croatian potatoes (see page 53), to serve

Dalmatian tomato sauce (see page 94), to serve

**This is a very popular way of preparing meat in Dalmatia. You can use many different cuts and varieties of meat. My mother usually prepares this dish with beef neck or ribs. After poaching the meat you will have a beautiful stock, which you can serve as a soup before the poached meat – just add some orzo pasta and cut vegetables from the stock to the soup and you have a great appetiser (see Note, below).**

Add the meat, vegetables, parsley and peppercorns to 3 litres (101 fl oz/ 12 cups) cold water in a saucepan and bring it to the boil. (Starting off with cold water will give a better flavour to the soup, but if you want the meat to be tastier, add the meat and the vegetables to boiling water.) Season with salt and let it simmer over low heat for 2–3 hours.

When the meat is cooked, take it out of the stock (reserve if making a soup – see Note, below) and cut it into smaller pieces. Season with more salt and drizzle with the olive oil. Serve with the potatoes and tomato sauce on the side.

**Note:** *For the soup, discard all the solid ingredients from the soup except the carrot and celeriac. Cut the carrot and celeriac into small pieces. Add some orzo pasta to the soup and cook until the pasta is al dente, about 5–10 minutes. Adjust the seasoning, drizzle with olive oil, sprinkle 1 tablespoon of parsley on top and serve.*

# Tripe

*Tripice*

SERVES 6

100 g (3½ oz) pancetta,
with lots of white fat
but no skin

4 garlic cloves, crushed

1–2 brown onions,
finely chopped

100 ml (3½ fl oz) extra-
virgin olive oil

1 carrot, finely chopped

2 celery stalks,
finely chopped

50 g (1¾ oz) prosciutto,
diced into 4 mm
(¼ in) cubes

400 ml (13½ fl oz) chicken
stock

125 ml (4 fl oz/½ cup)
tomato passata
(puréed tomatoes)

1 kg (2 lb 3 oz) cooked
tripe, cut into strips

2–3 waxy potatoes, such
as desiree, sebago or
nicola, sliced

3 tablespoons chopped
flat-leaf (Italian) parsley
(optional)

sea salt

freshly ground black
pepper

50 g (1¾ oz/½ cup) grated
parmesan, to serve

Tripe is almost a cult dish among Croatian foodies and lovers of gourmet cuisine. In Croatia, there are even tripe clubs that bring people together on the weekends to cook and enjoy this dish in a variety of ways. When I was a child, tripe was one of the most contentious things in the whole world. If you've ever smelt raw tripe cooking, you'll know why! My grandmother would blanch tripe for hours and the smell is very strong – I just hated it. But then, one night when I was 18 years old, I came home from a nightclub in the wee hours of the morning feeling ravenous. There was only tripe to eat. It tasted like pure heaven, and I was converted. Now sometimes I even dream of tripe – that's how much I love this dish. Tripe usually comes cooked from the butcher. Unless you have a pressure-cooker, I would not try to cook it from raw as it takes hours and has a very strong odour.

In a blender or food processor, blend the pancetta and garlic to a paste.

In a saucepan over high heat, sauté the onion in the olive oil until soft. Add the carrot and celery and cook for approximately 10 minutes or until soft. Add the prosciutto and sauté for a couple of minutes, then add the pancetta and garlic paste, chicken stock and tomato passata. Simmer for a couple of minutes over high heat, then add the tripe. Cover with water and cook for 10 minutes. Add the potato, more water or stock and season with salt and pepper. Simmer until the potatoes are cooked through. Sprinkle with parsley, if using, and parmesan and serve.

# Sweet and sour lamb kidneys

*Janjeći bubrezi na kiselo*

5 garlic cloves, crushed

100 ml (3½ fl oz) extra-
virgin olive oil

3 large brown onions,
thinly sliced

600 g (1 lb 5 oz) lamb
kidneys, washed
and cleaned

2 tablespoons
tomato paste
(concentrated purée)

200 ml (7 fl oz)
white wine

100 ml (3½ fl oz) prošek
(Dalmatian fortified
wine) or port

2 tablespoons sugar

2 tablespoons red
wine vinegar

2 tablespoons chopped
flat-leaf (Italian) parsley

sea salt

freshly ground black
pepper

•

**My mother is the master when it comes to preparing this dish and, as a child, it was one of my favourite things to eat. In Dalmatia, this is a popular way of preparing offal. Usually lamb offal is used for this dish. Polenta is always served with it, but mashed potato will do just as well.**

Heat the olive oil in a saucepan over high heat and sauté the garlic for few seconds, then add the onion and sauté for 10–15 minutes until translucent and golden brown. Add the whole kidneys, season well with salt and pepper and sauté for another 10 minutes.

Add the tomato paste and sauté for another minute or two. Add the wine and prošek, cover and cook on low heat for about an hour – the sauce should thicken and reduce.

In a small bowl, dissolve the sugar in the vinegar then add this mixture to the kidneys. Simmer, uncovered, for another 10 minutes. The sauce should be thick – if it's runny, cook it a little longer. Sprinkle with the chopped parsley and serve.

# Stuffed capsicums

*Punjene paprike*

SERVES 4–6

100 g (3½ oz) white bread
(no crust)

500 g (1 lb 2 oz) minced
(ground) beef

500 g (1 lb 2 oz) minced
(ground) lamb

4 tablespoons short-grain
white rice

1 small brown onion,
finely chopped

1 garlic clove,
finely chopped

1 tablespoon sweet or
hot paprika

2 teaspoons salt

1 teaspoon ground pepper

12 long capsicums
(bell peppers) or banana
chillies or 6 yellow
Hungarian peppers

1 litre (34 fl oz/4 cups)
Dalmatian tomato sauce
(see page 94)

500 ml (17 fl oz/2 cups)
vegetable stock

50 g (1¾ oz) pancetta or
prosciutto, cut into 1 cm
(½ in) thick slices

mashed potato, to serve
(optional)

•

**This is a classic recipe and one of the most popular dishes in Croatia. Traditionally we use Hungarian yellow peppers to make it, but these are hard to find in Australia. Instead, I recommend you use long capsicums (bell peppers) or banana chillies as they work really well in this recipe. This dish is usually prepared during the hot summer months when peppers are in season. It's braised and light on the stomach. I just love the flavour of tomato, capsicum and braised meat together. This dish is almost always served with mashed potatoes. It keeps well in the refrigerator for a few days and tastes even better the day after you have cooked it. Croatians usually cook a huge pot of stuffed capsicums, ready to be reheated and eaten a few times in the same week. Once you have cooked punjene paprike, it's very likely to become one of your favourite dishes.**

Soak the bread in a little water, then squeeze out any excess.

In another bowl, combine the minced beef and lamb, along with the bread, rice, onion, garlic, paprika, salt and pepper. Mix vigorously for a few minutes until well combined.

Cut a hole in the top of each capsicum and use a sharp knife to cut out the ribs and seeds. Be sure not to break the sides of the capsicum. Gently stuff the capsicum with the mince mixture.

Combine the tomato sauce with the vegetable stock in a large saucepan. If you are using capsicums or Hungarian peppers, arrange them upright and add the pancetta, otherwise place them in sideways if using banana chillies. Bring to the boil and simmer for 20–25 minutes on low heat. Serve with mashed potatoes, if desired.

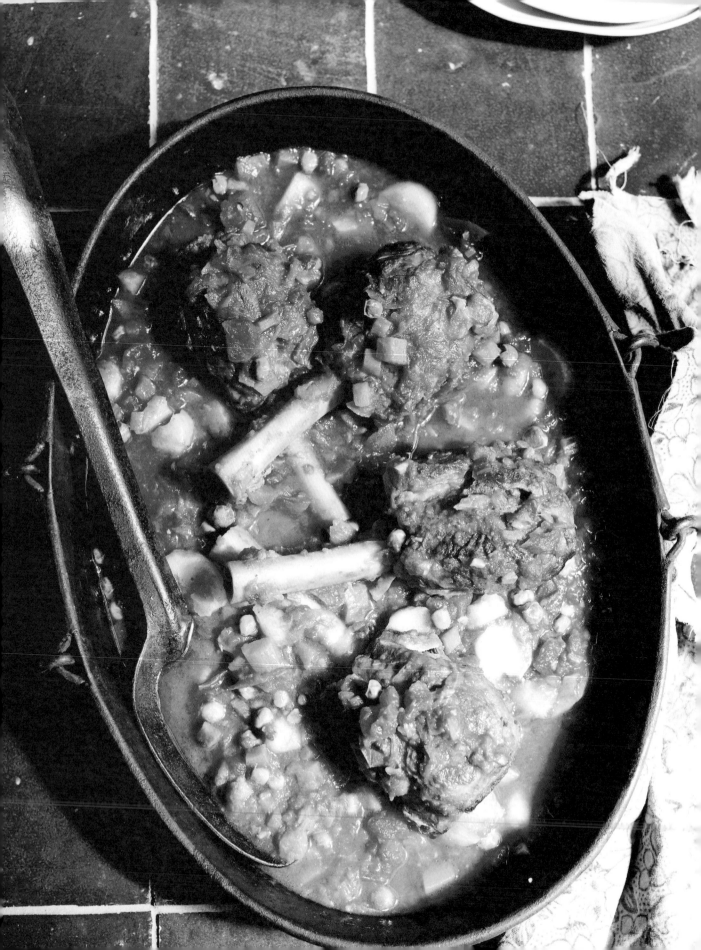

# Spring lamb stew
# with tomato and peas

*Janjetina s bižima*

SERVES 4

50 ml (1¾ fl oz) extra-
virgin olive oil

8 lamb shanks

4 garlic cloves, chopped

200 g (7 oz) brown
onions, chopped

200 g (7 oz) carrots, finely
diced

100 ml (3½ fl oz)
white wine

400 g (14 oz) tomatoes,
chopped

200 ml (7 fl oz) tomato
passata (puréed tomatoes)

200 ml (7 fl oz) chicken or
beef stock

2 bay leaves

200 g (7 oz) floury
potatoes, such as coliban
or king edward, diced into
2 cm (¾ in) cubes

700 g (1 lb 9 oz) fresh
or frozen baby peas

sea salt

freshly ground black
pepper

**What says spring better than the combination of lamb and baby peas? Even though this rich, classic dish is a favourite in springtime, it's wonderful all year round and perfect for any occasion. My mother loves to make this dish and I've based my recipe on hers – but I like to use whole shanks instead of diced lamb leg. You're guaranteed to find this dish on every table in Croatia's coastal regions of Dalmatia, Kvarner and Istria.**

Pour the olive oil into a large saucepan over high heat. Season the shanks well with salt and pepper, then sear them in the oil until they are nice and brown all over. Remove the lamb shanks from the pan and set aside on paper towel.

Add the garlic to the pan and fry for just a few seconds, making sure it doesn't burn. Add the onion – the onion will release water and stop the garlic from burning. Cook the onion on medium–low heat for about 10 minutes, then add the carrots and cook for another 10 minutes. Add the wine and cook until it evaporates, about 5 minutes.

Return the lamb shanks to the pan and add the tomato, passata, chicken stock and bay leaves. Adjust the seasoning and cook on low heat for 1 hour. Add the potatoes and peas and cook for another 20 minutes before serving.

# Potato dumplings with beef sauce
## *Valjušci od krumpira*

SERVES 4–6

sea salt

freshly ground black pepper

chopped flat-leaf (Italian)
parsley, to serve

freshly grated parmesan, to
serve

SAUCE

100 ml ($3\frac{1}{2}$ fl oz) extra-virgin
olive oil

1 kg (2 lb 3 oz) beef brisket,
cut into 1 cm ($\frac{1}{2}$ in) cubes

1 cinnamon stick

3 bay leaves

6 cloves

100 ml ($3\frac{1}{2}$ fl oz) white wine

2 tablespoons tomato paste
(concentrated purée)

1 kg (2 lb 3 oz) brown
onions, chopped

2 carrots, grated

200–400 ml ($7–13\frac{1}{2}$ fl oz)
chicken stock

POTATO DUMPLINGS

1 kg (2 lb 3 oz) waxy potatoes,
such as desiree, sebago or nicola

240 g ($8\frac{1}{2}$ oz) plain
(all-purpose) flour

50 g ($1\frac{3}{4}$ oz) butter, softened

1 egg

50 g ($1\frac{3}{4}$ oz/$\frac{1}{2}$ cup) grated
parmesan

**My grandmother was a dumpling specialist. I still remember rolling dumplings on the kitchen table while my grandmother watched the sauce on the stove. It's a special dish of my childhood, which brought me so much joy and happiness. I hope it will do the same for you. In Croatia we use potato dumplings with many different sauces, and this is one of the best. It is very important to use the right potatoes for dumplings – desiree is a good choice.**

Put half the olive oil in a large saucepan over high heat. When very hot, add the beef, cinnamon, bay leaves and cloves. Sauté until all the liquid evaporates from the beef and it starts to brown, about 20 minutes. It's important that the beef browns and there is caramelisation on both the beef and the bottom of the pan. Just before it starts to burn, add the white wine and tomato paste. Cook until the wine evaporates, another 5 minutes.

In a separate frying pan on low heat, sauté the onion in the remaining olive oil for 20 minutes. Add the carrot and cook until soft and sweet, about 10–15 minutes.

Add the onion and carrot mixture to the beef. Add half the stock and simmer over low heat, adding the rest of the stock gradually until the beef is tender, about 30 minutes.

For the dumplings, put the potatoes, unpeeled, in a saucepan of cold water. Season with salt and cook until the potatoes are soft and the tip of a knife can be easily inserted. Drain the potatoes and peel them while still hot.

Pass the potatoes through a potato ricer and put them in a bowl with the flour, softened butter, egg and parmesan and season with salt. Taste the dough to check if it's seasoned enough.

While still warm, roll the dough into 2 cm (¾ in) balls and roll a fork over them.

Cook the dumplings in boiling water for 3 minutes, until they come to the surface. Gently take them out of the pan with a slotted spoon, drain them, then put them in a bowl and pour the sauce over. Sprinkle with parsley and freshly grated parmesan and serve.

# Chicken and paprika stew
## *Pileći paprikaš*

SERVES 4

150 g (5½ oz) pancetta, diced

50 ml (1¾ fl oz) extra-virgin olive oil

3 brown onions, chopped

1 green capsicum (bell pepper), diced

1 tablespoon paprika

1 kg (2 lb 3 oz) chicken drumsticks

250 ml (8½ fl oz/1 cup) Dalmatian tomato sauce (see page 94)

250 ml (8½ fl oz/1 cup) chicken or vegetable stock

sea salt

freshly ground black pepper

POLENTA DUMPLINGS

250 g (9 oz/1⅔ cups) polenta

500 g (1 lb 2 oz) waxy potatoes, such as desiree, sebago or nicola

2 tablespoons olive oil or lard

•

**Dried paprika is used in many Croatian dishes. It is an essential ingredient in many smallgoods as well. This is a classic and very popular recipe. Chicken, paprika and tomato go beautifully together and if you make some polenta and potato dumplings to accompany your paprikaš, you are in for a real treat.**

In a saucepan over high heat, sauté the pancetta in the olive oil until translucent. Add the onion, capsicum and paprika, season well with salt and pepper and sauté for 5–10 minutes, until the onion starts to brown and the capsicum is soft. Then add the chicken drumsticks, turning them to coat. Cover with a lid and cook over low heat, turning the chicken occasionally, until all the liquid has evaporated and the chicken is a nice brown colour, about 30 minutes. Add the tomato sauce and chicken stock, and season with salt and pepper. Braise over low heat for another 20–30 minutes.

For the dumplings, bring 1.25 litres (42 fl oz/5 cups) of salted water to the boil, then whisk in the polenta. Boil over high heat for about 10 minutes, then reduce the heat to a simmer, stirring occasionally, and cook for about 50 minutes. (If you are using instant polenta, the cooking time is significantly shorter. Follow the packet instructions.)

In a separate saucepan, boil the potatoes in salted water until cooked. Mash them and add to the cooked polenta, mixing well to combine. Add the olive oil or lard and, while the polenta and potato mixture is still hot, use two spoons to shape it into quenelles. Serve with the paprikaš.

# Stuffed eggplant Dubrovnik-style

*Punjene balancane na dubrovački*

SERVES 4

4 eggplants (aubergines)

2 tablespoons dry breadcrumbs

50 ml (1¾ fl oz) extra-virgin oilve oil, plus extra for greasing and drizzling

100 g (3½ oz) minced (ground) beef

1 egg

50 g (1¾ oz) grated cheese (parmesan or similar)

100 g (3½ oz) prosciutto or ham, finely diced

500 ml (17 fl oz/2 cups) Dalmatian tomato sauce (see page 94)

1 bunch basil, chopped

sea salt

freshly ground black pepper

**In Croatia we have a custom of naming dishes after their town of origin. This dish certainly deserves to bear the name of Dubrovnik, one of the most beautiful towns in the Mediterranean.**

Cut the tops off the eggplants and set aside. Using a knife and spoon, hollow out the centres of the eggplants, leaving 1 cm (½ in) of flesh around the edge. Season the eggplants inside with salt and let them drain upside down for about 30 minutes – they will lose some bitterness this way.

In a frying pan over medium heat, sauté the breadcrumbs in the olive oil until golden brown. Remove the pan from the heat and set aside to cool.

In a bowl, mix the minced beef with the egg and cheese and season well.

Grease the insides of the eggplants with olive oil and start filling them first with the breadcrumbs then some of the beef mixture, some prosciutto and a tablespoon of Dalmatian tomato sauce. Sprinkle with chopped basil. Keep filling the eggplants in this order evenly (you should end up with three to four layers of each ingredient). When all the eggplants are filled, replace the eggplant tops.

Place the filled eggplants in a saucepan greased with olive oil. Add the remaining tomato sauce, 300 ml (10½ fl oz) water and drizzle with olive oil. Cook over low heat for about an hour, then serve.

# Veal stew

## *Žgvacet*

SERVES 4

800 g (1 lb 12 oz) veal meat (best from the leg), cut into 2 cm ($\frac{3}{4}$ in) cubes

100 g ($3\frac{1}{2}$ oz) lard

50 g ($1\frac{3}{4}$ oz/$\frac{1}{2}$ cup) dry breadcrumbs

1 brown onion, finely chopped

300 ml (10 fl oz) beef stock

$\frac{1}{2}$ nutmeg

100 g ($3\frac{1}{2}$ oz) grated cheese (parmesan or paški)

sea salt

freshly ground black pepper

$\frac{1}{4}$ cup chopped flat-leaf (Italian) parsley, to serve

**This is the traditional Dalmatian way of cooking veal stew. Just be sure to use young veal meat, which is still pale in colour. The meat quality is essential in this dish, as it contains only a few ingredients. It can be served with a variety of sides – baked rice, mashed potato and pasta are the most common.**

Put the veal in a dry saucepan over medium heat. Season with salt and pepper and cook the veal until all the liquid from the meat evaporates and starts to stick to the bottom of the pan, and the meat is a nice caramel colour – do not let it brown too much, though.

Put the lard in a separate saucepan over medium heat. Add the breadcrumbs and onion, season with salt and sauté until the onion becomes golden brown. Gradually add the beef stock to the onion and bring to the boil.

Add the stock and onion mixture to the meat and simmer over low heat until the stew thickens and the stock evaporates, about 30 minutes. Grate half a nutmeg over the meat, add the cheese and cook for a further 10 minutes. Adjust the seasoning, sprinkle with parsley and serve.

# Slow-cooked beef stew
# with prunes and apples
## *Pašticada*

SERVES 10

2.5 kg (5½ lb) beef cheeks

1 litre (34 fl oz/4 cups) red wine

50 ml (1¾ fl oz) red wine vinegar

2 onions, sliced 2 mm (⅛ in) thick

2 carrots, sliced 2 mm (⅛ in) thick

2 celery stalks, sliced 2 mm (⅛ in) thick

3 cloves

½ cinnamon stick

2 bay leaves

200 ml (7 fl oz) extra-virgin olive oil

100 g (3½ oz) prosciutto, chopped

3 garlic cloves, chopped

400 g (14 oz) tomatoes, cut into chunks

3 litres (101 fl oz/12 cups) beef stock

2 apples, peeled, cored and cut into wedges

200 g (7 oz) tinned pitted prunes, cut into 2–3 cm (¾–1¼ in) dice

1 tablespoon dijon mustard

1 teaspoon prune jam

sea salt

freshly ground black pepper

**This is the queen of Dalmatian dishes. It takes a long time to prepare – at least one day marinating in good red wine or prošek (Dalmatian fortified wine) and vegetables, and a good 3–4 hours' braising the next day. It's often served with potato dumplings (see page 152) or handmade pasta. In Dalmatia, pašticada is usually cooked for big celebrations. It's an essential dish for weddings, christenings or other equally important days. In Dalmatia you are considered a great cook if you can make this dish, and my grandmother Tomica was a pašticada expert. Don't be frightened by this though – it's not that hard; it just takes a little time. But don't forget the most important ingredient – love.**

Marinate the beef overnight in the red wine, vinegar, onion, carrot, celery, cloves, cinnamon and bay leaves.

The next day, take the beef out of the marinade, separating the vegetables and reserving the liquid.

Seal the cheeks in a frying pan in the olive oil over high heat for 2–3 minutes. Remove the beef from the pan and deglaze the pan with the liquid from the marinade.

In a saucepan over high heat, sauté the chopped prosciutto and, when crispy, the chopped garlic. Add all the marinated vegetables and spices and sauté for 20–25 minutes.

When the vegetables are cooked, add the tomato and sauté for a further 5 minutes.

Add the sealed beef cheeks, the liquid you used to deglaze the pan and the beef stock. Braise for 1½ hours. Add the peeled apples and pitted prunes and cook for a further hour or until the cheeks are cooked – you should be able to push your finger through the cheek but it should still have some resistance.

When the beef cheeks are cooked, remove the beef, cinnamon stick and bay leaves from the braising liquid and set aside. Skim the scum from the top of the liquid, then blend it with a hand-held blender until smooth.

Adjust the flavour by adding the mustard and prune jam – the flavour should be sweet and sour. Divide the beef cheeks among serving plates and pour the sauce over to serve.

# Poached beef tongue with caper salsa
## *Gođeđi jezik s kaparima*

SERVES 4

sea salt
freshly ground black pepper

POACHED TONGUE

1 beef tongue (500–800 g
/1 lb 2 oz–1 lb 12 oz)

100 g ($3\frac{1}{2}$ oz) pancetta, cut
into 5 mm ($\frac{1}{4}$ in) strips

100 g ($3\frac{1}{2}$ oz) pork skin

1 veal bone or shank,
approximately 250 g (9 oz)

3 carrots, roughly chopped

1 turnip, roughly chopped

2 celery stalks, roughly
chopped

1 bay leaf

1 brown onion, diced

3–4 cloves

5–6 peppercorns

100 ml ($3\frac{1}{2}$ fl oz) white wine
or port

CAPER SALSA

100 g ($3\frac{1}{2}$ oz) capers

100 g ($3\frac{1}{2}$ oz) gherkins (dill
pickles), chopped into small
cubes (the same size as
the capers)

$\frac{1}{2}$ red onion, chopped

2 tablespoons chopped
flat-leaf (Italian) parsley

50 ml ($1\frac{3}{4}$ fl oz) extra-virgin
olive oil

25 ml ($\frac{3}{4}$ fl oz) red wine vinegar

**In Croatia there are many ways of preparing beef tongue and it's often used as a part of cured salami, or pickled with various herbs and spices. This is something a little different to serve as an appetiser for your guests. Don't tell them what it is until they try it – this will ensure that they actually give it a chance! I often put this dish on the specials board in my restaurant and, even though it's not a big seller, there are plenty of people who absolutely love it.**

Pierce the tongue with a sharp knife and push the pieces of pancetta into the cuts. Place the tongue in a large saucepan and cover well with water. Add all the remaining tongue ingredients and season with salt. Simmer over low heat for about 2–3 hours, until the tongue can be easily pierced with a fork.

Remove the tongue from the water (reserving a few spoonfuls of the cooking water), allow to cool, then peel the skin off the tongue. Slice the tongue into thin slices and arrange on a serving platter.

For the caper salsa, mix all the ingredients together, season with salt and pepper and add the reserved stock in which the tongue was cooked. Spread the salsa over the warm tongue, let it cool slightly, then serve.

# Dalmatian steak

*Pržolica*

SERVES 4

4 beef steaks (T-bone
or porterhouse)

3 waxy potatoes, such as
desiree, sebago or nicola,
peeled and sliced

3 garlic cloves, finely
chopped

100 ml (3½ fl oz) extra-
virgin olive oil

1 brown onion, sliced

500 g (1 lb 2 oz) silverbeet
(Swiss chard), cut into
strips

2 large tomatoes, cut
into cubes

50 ml (1¾ fl oz)
white wine

sea salt

freshly ground black
pepper

**This is a traditional way to serve steak in Dalmatia. We aren't big fans
of chips (French fries) and, for some reason, we love to eat silverbeet
(Swiss chard) instead with most of our dishes – it's definitely the most
popular side dish. Could this be the reason why Dalmatians are some of
the tallest people in Europe?**

Preheat a barbecue grill plate or chargrill pan to high heat then grill the
steaks to your liking. After barbecuing, season the steaks with salt and
pepper. Rest the steaks in a warm place (on top of the barbecue or in a
150°C/300°F oven) for 5–10 minutes before serving.

Cook the potatoes in boiling salted water for about 10 minutes. Remove
the saucepan from the heat.

In a large frying pan over medium heat, sauté the garlic in the olive oil
for 2–3 seconds, making sure it doesn't start to colour. Add the sliced onion
and sauté for about 5 minutes. Add the silverbeet, tomatoes and white wine.
Cook for about 10 minutes until everything has combined well and the
wine has evaporated.

Strain the cooked potatoes and add them to the pan, along with a little
of the potato cooking water to add moisture. Cook for another 5 minutes.
Serve the silverbeet and potato mixture with the grilled steak.

# Beef and pork wrapped in vine leaves
*Sinjski arambašići*

SERVES 6

600 g (1 lb 5 oz) beef (neck or chuck steak)

150 g (5½ oz) pancetta

50 g (1¾ oz) beef fat (from the butcher)

200 g (7 oz) pork meat (neck or shoulder)

2 large brown onions, finely chopped

4 garlic cloves, finely chopped

zest of 1 lemon

1 teaspoon cinnamon

pinch of ground cloves

¼ nutmeg

300 g (10½ oz) preserved vine leaves

200 g (7 oz) Sauerkraut (page 52)

1 tablespoon lard

200 g (7 oz) smoked pork ribs

50 g (1¾ oz) prosciutto (optional), cut into 1 cm (½ in) slices (optional)

100 g (3½ oz) dried goat (if you can't find it use extra pork ribs) (optional)

400 ml (13½ fl oz) chicken or vegetable stock

sea salt

freshly ground black pepper

**Arambašići is a speciality from the town of Sinj in the Dalmatian hinterland. The dish is clearly Turkish or Middle Eastern in origin, but the use of pork in this version makes it very Croatian. The town of Sinj was on the border of the Ottoman Empire and has changed hands several times during its turbulent history. On 25 September 1686, the Croatians and Venetians liberated Sinj from Turkish rule. I'm proud to say that the first flag put on the Sinj fortress that day was a Saint George flag from my ancestral village of Gata, once the centre of the proud Poljička Republika (an independent Croatian state at that time). The Turks must have left their arambašići still warm on the stove, and the Croatians took a liking to the dish, as it is still prepared in Dalmatia to this day. To make tasty arambašići you need to have good-quality sauerkraut. I have suggested making your own, but if you buy store-bought, make sure it's a quality product. Serve it as a main course with some mashed potato.**

Using a large knife or cleaver, chop the beef, pancetta, beef fat and pork into small pieces – it will taste much better if you chop it by hand, instead of mincing (grinding) it.

Put the chopped meat in a large bowl. Add the onion, garlic, lemon zest, cinnamon, cloves and grate over the nutmeg. Mix well with your hands for a few minutes.

Separate the vine leaves and rinse them with water. Rinse the sauerkraut.

Place a vine leaf on a work surface and place a tablespoon of the meat mixture in the centre. Fold up the sides and roll into a tight parcel. Repeat with the remaining vine leaves.

Put the lard in the bottom of a clay pot or heavy-based saucepan, then add a layer of sauerkraut. Add a layer of arambašići, placed tightly next to each other. Add some more sauerkraut and the smoked pork ribs – you can add the prosciutto and dried goat for more flavour, if desired. Add another layer of arambašići then add more sauerkraut on top. Cover with chicken stock and cook over low heat for 3–4 hours, shaking the pan occasionally and adding more stock if needed.

# Pork, pasta and bean soup
## *Pašta fažol*

SERVES 4

500 g (1 lb 2 oz) beans
(cannellini/lima or
borlotti/cranberry)

4 bay leaves

200 g (7 oz) smoked pork
shanks or ribs

2 litres (68 fl oz/8 cups)
water or beef stock

200 g (7 oz) brown
onions, chopped

2 carrots, chopped

4 celery stalks, chopped

2 tablespoons tomato
paste (concentrated
purée)

150 g (5 ½ oz) smoked
pancetta with lots of
white fat (must be flat
and smoked)

8 garlic cloves

100 g (3 ½ oz) pasta
(penne or small tubetti)

sea salt

freshly ground black
pepper

2 tablespoons chopped
flat-leaf (Italian) parsley,
to garnish

**Pašta fažol is by far Croatia's most popular dish. Continental Croatians call this hearty dish 'grah', but don't include pasta. However, in Dalmatia, the dish is a more Mediterranean version. This rich soup is a soul-warmer and you can serve it as an appetiser or as the main meal with fresh, crusty bread and a good Dalmatian wine. The secret ingredient to making this delicious meal is the pancetta fat and garlic paste. It's crucial to soak the dried beans overnight then blanch them in water to remove the toxins – your stomach will thank you!**

Soak the beans overnight. The following day, drain them and put them in a large saucepan with the bay leaves. Cover with water and bring to the boil. Drain the water from the pan. Don't season the beans yet.

In another large saucepan, put the pork shanks, water or stock, vegetables, tomato paste and the red meat trimmed from the pancetta. Bring to the boil then reduce the heat to low. Season with salt and pepper. Simmer for 1 hour until the vegetables are soft.

Meanwhile, finely chop the white fat part of the pancetta and blend it in a food processor with the garlic to make a smooth paste.

After the soup has been cooking for 1 hour, remove the pancetta meat and pork bones and add the blanched beans and garlic and fat paste. Simmer for another 30 minutes until the beans are soft and starting to break up.

If you want to thicken the soup, scoop out a couple of cups of the soup (including vegetables and meat), blend in a food processor, then return this to the pan before adding the pasta.

Add the pasta and cook for another 5 minutes, adding more water or stock if necessary. Garnish with parsley and serve.

# Pork skewers

*Ražnjići*

**Ražnjići is a very popular barbecued dish in Croatia that originated in the Middle East or Asia, but somehow found its way to Croatian tables. You can use beef or lamb instead of pork and even some bacon to make it more flavoursome. It's delicious served with Sautéed vegetables with rice, or đuveđ (page 46).**

Slice the pork neck into 1 cm (½ in) slices and then into 3 cm (1¼ in) cubes.

For the marinade, combine the onion and garlic in a mixing bowl with the herbs, olive oil, vinegar and salt and pepper. Add the meat, eggplant and capsicum. Mix well to combine then leave in the refrigerator overnight.

The following day, cut the onions into large slices and start spiking the marinated meat, onion, eggplant and capsicum onto skewers. (You can use metal or wooden skewers – if you use wooden ones, make sure you soak them in water for an hour first so they don't burn on the barbecue.)

Preheat a barbecue grill plate or chargrill pan to high.

Grill the skewers on the barbecue for about 5 minutes on each side or until the meat is cooked through. Squeeze over some lemon juice, drizzle with olive oil and serve.

SERVES 4

800 g (1 lb 12 oz) pork neck

1 eggplant (aubergine), cut into 3 cm (1¼ in) dice

2 capsicums (bell peppers), cut into 3 cm (1¼ in) dice

2 brown onions

juice of ½ lemon

extra-virgin olive oil, for drizzling

sea salt

freshly ground black pepper

MARINADE

1 brown onion, chopped

4 garlic cloves, chopped

2 rosemary sprigs

10 thyme sprigs

2 bay leaves

100 ml (3½ fl oz) extra-virgin olive oil

30 ml (1 fl oz) white wine vinegar

# Peka

*Peka*

50 ml (1¾ fl oz) vegetable or olive oil

100 g (3½ oz) lard

400 g (14 oz) waxy potatoes, such as desiree, sebago or nicola, sliced

6 shallots, halved

4 garlic cloves, chopped

1 eggplant (aubergine), thickly sliced

2 capsicums (bell peppers), halved

1 rosemary sprig

1 kg (2 lb 3 oz) meat for roasting (beef, veal, chicken or lamb) in one piece

**This is a very specific way of cooking, found only in Croatia. Most of the Croatians have a *komin* – an outdoor, open wood-fired oven with bricks on the bottom and a peka (a cast-iron bell-shaped cover) hanging next to it. A peka is also used to bake a special kind of bread we call brašenica, and seafood can also be baked under a peka – most famously, octopus. We light a fire on the brick bottom and, when the wood or coal is burned and only hot coal is left, we start to cook. If you don't have all this equipment, you can just use your oven and cover the baking tray with aluminium foil. It will still taste great but won't have that special smoky flavour of true peka.**

Grease a round roasting tin with the oil and lard. Place the vegetables and rosemary in the tin and the meat on top.

If you are using a wood-fired oven, put the roasting tin on the hot bricks in the oven then cover the tin with the metal peka. Cover the peka with the hot coal and ashes from the burnt wood and cook for 1 hour.

Remove the coal and ashes and open the peka to check it. Gently mix the vegetables and turn the meat so everything is evenly cooked and coloured. Cover with the peka and the coal and ashes again and cook for a further 20–30 minutes. It should take about 1½ hours to cook all together. If the meat is still not tender, cook it for a bit longer.

**Note:** *If you don't have a peka or a wood-fired oven, you can cook the meat and the vegetables in a regular oven. Place the meat and all the other ingredients in a heavy baking tin and cover with foil. Bake at 220°C (430°F) for about 1½ hours. Remove the foil for the last 20 minutes to get a nice golden brown colour on the meat.*

*To make octopus peka, replace the meat with the same quantity of octopus. Tenderise the octopus by freezing it for 2–3 days, then defrost it completely and beat it all over with a mallet or rolling pin to break down the muscles. Before roasting, it will need to be boiled for 10 minutes in unseasoned water (the octopus is very salty). The potatoes should be cut into 1 cm (½ in) slices. Place the vegetables in the tin with the boiled octopus on top and season the vegetables only. Bake at 220°C (430°F) for 45 minutes.*

chapter four

# SWEETS

.

•

# In Croatia we like to save the best until last and, of course, every great meal needs its sweet ending.

Throughout history, Croatia has been at the crossroads of many cultures and cuisines: from the Habsburg Empire with its layered pastries rich with cream, chocolate and custard; the Mediterranean with its figs and deep-fried treats; to the mystical flavours of the east filled with the aroma of heady spices. With so many influences it's hard to determine which desserts actually originated in Croatia. However, we can be sure that the maraschino liqueur of Zadar is definitely one of our own contributions to the world's great pastry shop.

In Croatia we like to save the best until last and, of course, every great meal needs its sweet ending. In this chapter, I have selected some recipes that my family makes at home and which are close to my heart.

The most popular dessert in Croatia is probably palačinke, or pancakes. These can be served many different ways, such as filled with plum jam or a walnut and cream mixture, or simply sprinkled with lemon juice and sugar. Fritule are small doughnuts that are always made for Christmas and Easter in the coastal areas of Croatia. These are often served as a welcome to the celebration along with a shot of rakija, a brandy made from wine or pressed grapes. Strudel and knedle (dumplings filled with cherries or plums) are also popular desserts, and walnut and poppy seed roulade is a much-loved classic often seen in Croatian households.

Many towns in Croatia have their own sweet recipe, which they treasure. Dubrovnik prides itself on its rožata, a version of créme caramel, while Hvar is famous for its paprenjaci, or spicy pepper biscuits. The beautiful ancient town of Trogir is known for its rafioli, which are similar to savoury ravioli in that they are small pockets of dough, but they are filled with a nut and spice-laced chocolate mixture.

•

# Bombiće

*Bombiće*

SERVES 8

The name 'bombiće' is very apt, as these are little bombs of flavour. They should be dried for a few days before eating. However, the only problem is that in my house they never last that long as they're so delicious! Serve them with coffee or tea in the afternoon or for any other sweet occasion. Below are four variations.

## Chocolate

### CHOCOLATE

200 g (7 oz) butter, softened

150 g (5½ oz) caster (superfine) sugar

finely grated zest of 1 orange

pinch of ground cloves

1 tablespoon dark rum

200 g (7 oz) crushed biscuits (any good-quality plain biscuits)

100 g (3½ oz) dark chocolate, grated

Using an electric mixer, cream the butter and sugar until light and fluffy. Mix in the orange zest, cloves, rum and crushed biscuits. When everything is well combined, roll the mixture into 2 cm (¾ in) balls. Roll the balls in the grated chocolate then leave them on a tray overnight, or longer, to dry. Transfer to decorative paper cases before serving, if desired.

## Dried fig

### DRIED FIG

250 g (9 oz) dried figs

finely grated zest and juice of 1 orange

60 g (2 oz) almonds, chopped

2 tablespoons dark rum

50 g (1¾ oz) dark chocolate

120 g (4½ oz) icing (confectioners') sugar

100 g (3½ oz) caster (superfine) sugar, for rolling

In a saucepan bring 1 litre (34 fl oz/4 cups) water to the boil then drop in the figs. Blanch them for 30 seconds, then drain, rinse in cold water and dry with paper towel. Transfer to a food processor and blend to a paste. Mix in the orange zest and half its juice, the chopped almonds, rum, grated chocolate and icing sugar. When everything is well combined, roll the mixture into 2 cm (¾ in) balls. Roll the balls in the caster sugar and dry for a day or two. Transfer to decorative paper cases before serving, if desired.

Continued ...

## CHESTNUT

500 g (1 lb 2 oz) chestnuts

250 g (9 oz) caster
(superfine) sugar

2 tablespoons maraschino
liqueur

1 tablespoon dark rum

100 g (3½ oz) grated dark
chocolate

## Chestnut

Places the chestnuts in a saucepan of cold water, bring to the boil, cover and simmer for 15–20 minutes or until the flesh is tender. Drain the chestnuts and transfer them to a tea towel (dish towel). While they are still warm (chestnuts are difficult to peel once cool), remove the outer shell and inner skin.

Crush the chestnuts into a smooth paste in a food processor or using a potato ricer. Add the sugar, maraschino and rum and blend with the chestnut paste. Form 2 cm (¾ in) balls from the mixture and roll them in the grated chocolate. Place them in decorative paper cases, if desired, and dry at room temperature for a few days before serving.

## CARROT

500 g (1 lb 2 oz) carrots,
peeled and grated

250 g (9 oz) caster
(superfine) sugar, plus
extra for rolling

zest of 3 oranges

## Carrot

In a saucepan over low heat, cook the grated carrot, sugar and orange zest until the mixture thickens. It should still be moist so you can form balls. Leave the mixture to cool. Form 2 cm (¾ in) balls from the mixture and roll them in sugar. Place them in decorative paper cases and dry at room temperature for a few days before serving.

# Bobići

*Bobići*

SERVES 8

900 g (2 lb/6 cups) almonds

6 eggs

700 g (1 lb 9 oz) caster (superfine) sugar

1 teaspoon baking powder

1 nutmeg, freshly grated

zest of 1 lemon

30 ml (1 fl oz) maraschino liqueur

50 g (1¾ oz) dark chocolate, grated

50 g (1¾ oz) biscuits, crushed (any good-quality plain biscuits)

50 g (1¾ oz) natural beeswax

•

**In my home town of Split, there is a great pastry shop that makes these sweet treats and sells them by the kilogram. Many times on my way home from school I would go and buy a small paper bag full of these brown and white delights. They are easy to make and keep for a few months in a jar.**

Put half the almonds in a food processor and blitz to a paste. Chop the remaining almonds with a knife into large pieces.

Using an electric mixer, beat the eggs with the sugar until pale in colour. With the machine running on medium speed, add the almond paste and chopped almonds, baking powder, grated nutmeg, lemon zest and maraschino liqueur. Mix until well combined and then divide the mixture in half. To one half add the grated chocolate and to the other the biscuit crumbs. Mix in using a spatula. Once the ingredients are well combined, divide both halves of the dough into thumb-sized balls.

Wrap the natural beeswax in muslin (cheesecloth).

Preheat the oven to 140°C (275°F).

Warm a baking tray and grease it with the beeswax wrapped in the cloth. Place the bobići on the baking tray and press each one with your fingertip to make a small indentation. Bake for around 30 minutes or until cooked. Test one by breaking it in half – it should be dry in the centre. Cool on a wire rack before storing in a sealed jar.

# Pancakes

*Palačinke*

Palačinke arc a vcry popular central European dessert. They're a once-a-week must on any Croatian table. In fact, walnut and chocolate palačinke are one of the most popular dishes in Croatian restaurants. The French make a very similar dish called crêpes – although the original recipe came from Hungary and is called gundel palacsinta. It is made with a ground walnut, raisin, candied orange peel, cinnamon and rum filling, served flambéed in a dark chocolate sauce. I have provided a simpler recipe designed to make at home in 20 minutes. If you want a shortcut, you can use chocolate and hazelnut spread instead of chocolate sauce.

## Ricotta pancakes with strawberry compote

For the cheese filling, roughly chop the almonds. Put them in a bowl, add the remaining filling ingredients and gently work into a paste.

For the pancakes, place the flour, eggs, milk, sugar and salt in a food processor or blender. Add the melted butter. Blend until smooth, then strain into a jug. Cover and set aside to rest for 30 minutes at room temperature.

Dip a piece of paper towel in the canola oil and use it to brush the base of a 16 cm (6¼ in) non-stick frying pan set over medium heat. When the oil is hot, pour in just enough batter to cover the base. Tilt the pan so the batter completely covers the base in a thin film and pour any excess back into the jug. Cook the pancake for about 1 minute until the underside is golden, then use a metal spatula to flip it over. Cook the other side for just under a minute, until golden. Transfer to a plate and cover with foil to keep warm. Repeat with the remaining pancake mixture.

For the strawberry compote, combine the sugar with 50 ml (1¾ fl oz) water in a saucepan and heat to 118°C (244°F). However, be careful not to caramelise the sugar, as it needs to be clear and thick. As soon as the sugar is ready, add the strawberries, vanilla seeds and lemon juice. Bring to the boil and immediately remove the pan from the heat. Don't overcook the strawberries or they will lose colour, flavour and become too soft. Leave the mixture to cool then store in the refrigerator until serving.

To assemble the palačinke, preheat the oven to 180°C (350°F).

Spread 2 or 3 tablespoons of the cheese filling onto each palačinke, then fold or roll them. Grease a baking dish with butter, place the palačinke in the dish and cover with aluminium foil. Bake for 10 minutes. Remove the foil, pour the strawberry compote over the palačinke and serve with ice cream, if desired.

SERVES 8

PANCAKE BATTER

150 g (5½ oz/1 cup) plain (all-purpose) flour

2 eggs

200 ml (7 fl oz) milk

1 teaspoon caster (superfine) sugar

pinch of salt

50 g (1¾ oz) unsalted butter, melted

100 ml (3½ fl oz) canola oil

ice cream, to serve (optional)

CHEESE FILLING

100 g (3½ oz/⅔ cup) roasted almonds

400 g (14 oz) Bjelovarac (or ricotta)

50 g (1¾ oz) caster (superfine) sugar

1 teaspoon grated lemon zest

STRAWBERRY COMPOTE

100 g (3½ oz) caster (superfine) sugar

250 g (9 oz) fresh strawberries, washed, hulled and halved

1 cm (½ in) vanilla bean, split and seeds scraped

50 ml (1¾ fl oz) lemon juice

200 g (7 oz) walnuts

50 g (1¾ oz) caster (superfine) sugar

2 tablespoons raisins

1 teaspoon grated orange zest

100 ml (3½ fl oz) whipped cream

pinch of salt

CHOCOLATE SAUCE

200 ml (7 fl oz) thick (heavy/double) cream

50 ml (1¾ fl oz) milk

200 g (7 oz) dark chocolate, chopped

20 g (¾ oz) unsweetened (Dutch) cocoa powder

## Walnut pancakes with chocolate sauce

Follow the pancake batter recipe for Ricotta pancakes with strawberry compote (opposite).

To make the walnut filling, roughly chop the walnuts. Put them in a bowl, add all the other ingredients and gently work into a paste.

For the chocolate sauce, combine the cream and milk in a saucepan over medium heat and bring to just below boiling point. Remove the pan from the heat and gently whisk in the chocolate and cocoa until smooth. Set aside to cool. (Extra sauce will keep refrigerated for up to 5 days.)

To assemble the palačinke, spread 2 tablespoons of the walnut filling onto each palačinke, then fold or roll them. Serve them warm with the chocolate sauce drizzled over.

# Little doughnuts
*Fritule*

SERVES 6

500 g (1 lb 2 oz) waxy potatoes, such as desiree, sebago or nicola

zest of 1 lemon

zest of 1 orange

pinch of freshly grated nutmeg

1 cm ($\frac{1}{2}$ in) vanilla bean, split and seeds scraped

50 ml ($1\frac{3}{4}$ fl oz) dark rum

40 g ($1\frac{1}{2}$ oz) caster (superfine) sugar, plus extra for rolling

2 eggs, whisked

200 g (7 oz/$1\frac{1}{3}$ cups) plain (all-purpose) flour

5 g ($\frac{1}{4}$ oz) instant yeast

50 g ($1\frac{3}{4}$ oz) sultanas (golden raisins), soaked in 50 ml ($1\frac{3}{4}$ fl oz) dark rum for 30 minutes

1 teaspoon grappa

oil for deep-frying (canola or cottonseed)

•

**I associate this small doughnut-like sweet with some of my most joyful memories, as it is a Croatian festive food. Every celebration in Mediterranean Croatia starts with fritule, dried figs and rakija (grape brandy). One of my most profound memories is the smell of fritule on Christmas Day and my grandmother standing at the stove. For me, fritule represent pure joy – an essential ingredient and part of our culture. There are many recipe variations for this sweet and they are passed down through the generations. Every village and town in Dalmatia and Istria has its own recipe, which they claim is the original and the best. This one is made with potatoes and works really well. Serve fritule with dried figs and a fruit brandy, such as rakija or travarica, at the start of a celebration, as they are more of a welcoming sweet dish than a dessert.**

Place the potatoes in a saucepan. Cover with cold water and bring to the boil over high heat. Cook for 20–25 minutes or until just tender when tested with a skewer (don't test too often or the potatoes will become waterlogged). Drain well and set aside until just cool enough to handle. While still hot, peel and discard the skins.

Using a potato ricer, purée the potatoes into a bowl. While they are still warm, add the lemon and orange zest, nutmeg, vanilla seeds, rum, sugar and whisked eggs. Mix in the flour and yeast, then add the sultanas soaked in rum and the grappa. Mix everything together and add a little water. Stir until the mixture is smooth and shiny. Set aside to stand for 1 hour.

Heat the oil in a deep-fryer or deep frying pan until it reaches 180°C (350°F), or when a cube of bread dropped into the oil browns in 10 seconds. Scoop up about a thumb-sized piece of the dough, and squeeze and shape it into a small ball. Dip a teaspoon into cold oil to stop the dough from sticking, then use the teaspoon to pick up a ball of dough and drop it into the hot oil. Fry until golden brown, about 3–5 minutes. Repeat with the remaining dough balls. Remove the fritule from the fryer and drain on paper towel. Roll in caster sugar and serve.

# Peaches

*Breskvice*

**These are beautiful, tasty little pastries, which look like peaches. I remember how my aunt loved to make them. Still to this day I can see my aunt's Czech crystal bowl full of peaches and my mum warning me not to eat too many. They are very popular all through Central Europe, and it's hard to determine their country of origin.**

To make the dough, beat the eggs and sugar in an electric mixer until pale. Using a spatula, gently stir in the vegetable oil, 4 tablespoons of flour and the baking powder. Set aside to prove for 4 hours.

Add the remaining flour and the salt, and mix with your hands until you have a smooth dough.

Preheat the oven to 180°C (350°F).

Roll the dough into 2.5 cm (1 in) balls, place on a greased baking tray and bake for about 10–15 minutes until they are light and firm. Set aside to cool.

Using a small knife, cut a small hole in the bottom of the pastries and scoop out a little of the centre.

Crush the pastry from the centres into small crumbs (you can do it in a food processor).

For the filling, mix the pastry crumbs with the apricot jam, rum and almonds. Fill the hollow pastry shells with the filling and join two balls together to form a 'peach'. (The two balls will flatten slightly to look like two halves of a peach.)

Dip both sides of the pastries in the strawberry extract and pear liqueur, then in the water and then roll them in the sugar. Press cloves into the tops of the peaches to resemble stems.

SERVES 8

DOUGH

4 eggs

250 g (9 oz) caster (superfine) sugar

300 ml (10 fl oz) vegetable oil

1 kg (2 lb 3 oz/6⅔ cups) plain (all-purpose) flour

1 teaspoon baking powder

1 teaspoon salt

150 g (5½ oz) apricot jam

2 tablespoons dark rum

50 g (1¾ oz/⅓ cup) almonds, finely chopped

DECORATION

2 tablespoons strawberry or cherry extract

4 tablespoons kruškovac (Croatian pear liqueur) or dark rum

300 ml (10 fl oz) cold water

100 g (3½ oz) caster (superfine) sugar

cloves, for the stems

# Pear strudel

*Štrudla od kruške*

SERVES 6

115 g (4 oz/½ cup) caster
(superfine) sugar

1 kg (2 lb 3 oz) pears,
peeled, cored and diced
into 1 cm (½ in) cubes

1 tablespoon lemon juice

40 ml kruškovac
(Croatian pear liqueur),
dark rum or calvados

95 g (3¼ oz/½ cup)
brown sugar

200 g (7 oz) butter, melted

100 g (3½ oz) sponge
fingers (savoiardi/
lady fingers) or any
other similar biscuit,
roughly crushed

100 g (3½ oz) walnuts, crushed

95 g (¼ oz/½ cup) chopped
dried figs

1 teaspoon ground
cinnamon

¼ teaspoon freshly
grated nutmeg

60 g (2 oz/⅓ cup) sultanas
(golden raisins)

12 sheets filo pastry

50 g (1¾ oz/½ cup) dry
breadcrumbs

olive oil spray

icing (confectioners')
sugar, for dusting

chocolate sauce, to serve
(optional)

ice cream, to serve
(optional)

**Strudel is a Central European dessert with Hungarian origins. Since Croatia was once a part of the Habsburg Empire, it's a favourite national dish for us as well. There are many versions and techniques in making strudel. One classic filling is apple and sour (morello) cherry, but you can also use savoury flavours, such as goat's cheese, spinach or ricotta. Most people in Croatia make their own pastry, but you can also use pre-made puff pastry. Pear strudel is a favourite of mine, and it goes very well with chocolate, so I recommend serving it with a chocolate sauce (see page 181). Ice cream is also good served on the side.**

Preheat a large frying pan over high heat and, when it is very hot, add the sugar and allow it to melt and caramelise for 2–3 minutes or until it turns a deep golden brown. Add the diced pears and lemon juice. Sauté quickly and stir with a metal spoon for about 5 minutes, then add the kruškovac. Remove the pan from the stove.

In a food processor, place one-third of the sautéed pears, all of the brown sugar and half the melted butter. Purée until smooth. Stir this mixture back into the remaining pears. Add the crushed sponge fingers, crushed walnuts, dried figs, cinnamon, nutmeg and sultanas. Mix until well combined then set aside to cool.

Place a sheet of filo pastry on a work surface and brush with the remaining melted butter. Sprinkle with 1 tablespoon of the breadcrumbs. Top with another sheet of filo pastry and continue to layer with filo and breadcrumbs until you have six layers.

Spoon half the pear mixture along the length of the filo, leaving a 3 cm (1¼ in) border at the short ends.

Fold the ends in and roll the strudel up, lifting it carefully onto a baking tray. Repeat with the remaining sheets of filo and the rest of the fruit. Spray with olive oil and bake for 25 minutes, or until the pastry is golden. Allow to stand for 10 minutes. Slice and dust with icing sugar. Serve the strudel with chocolate sauce and ice cream, if desired.

# Chocolate knedle

*Knedle od čokolade*

**Knedle are a Central European dessert, Austrian in origin. Usually they are made with plums, but this is my own version. You could use many different fillings, as well as different sauces. Strawberries and cherries are very nice in knedle, and they are delicious served hot with ice cream and a few pieces of sticky candied orange on the side.**

For the dough, cook the potatoes in their skins in boiling water. Allow the potatoes to cool completely, then peel and pass through a potato ricer into a large mixing bowl. Mix in the softened butter, flour, egg and a pinch of salt. Shape the potato mixture into balls measuring 1.5 cm (½ in) in diameter, then set aside.

Make the ganache by heating the orange syrup in a saucepan over low heat until the temperature reaches 80°C (176°F), using a sugar thermometer to check the temperature. Remove the pan from the heat and fold in the melted chocolate until the mixture is smooth. Stir in the butter, mix well and allow to cool. Once the mixture has cooled and thickened, shape the chocolate ganache into balls measuring 1.5 cm (½ in) in diameter, then set aside.

For the crumb, cook the breadcrumbs in the ghee in a frying pan over medium heat until golden brown. Allow to cool then stir in the sugar.

When you're ready to cook the dumplings, push the chocolate ganache balls into the centre of the potato balls and shape the dough around them so the chocolate is completely enclosed in the dough. Cook the dumplings in boiling water for 4 minutes, then remove and dip the balls into the breadcrumb and sugar mixture. Serve hot with ice cream, if desired.

SERVES 4

ice cream, to serve
(optional)

DOUGH

500 g (1 lb 2 oz) waxy
potatoes, such as desiree,
sebago or nicola

50 g (1¾ oz) butter,
softened

160 g (5½ oz) plain
(all-purpose) flour

1 egg

pinch of salt

GANACHE

50 ml (1¼ fl oz)
orange syrup

500 g (1 lb 2 oz) dark
chocolate, melted

50 g (1¾ oz) butter

CRUMB

100 g (3½ oz/1 cup)
dry breadcrumbs

50 g (1¾ oz) ghee

50 g (1¾ oz) caster
(superfine) sugar

# Croatian apple cake
*Kolač od jabuke*

SERVES 6

375 g (13 oz/2$\frac{1}{2}$ cups) plain (all-purpose) flour

1 tablespoon baking powder

165 g (5$\frac{1}{2}$ oz) butter

165 g (5$\frac{1}{2}$ oz) caster (superfine) sugar

1 egg

zest of 1 lemon

2 tablespoons dark rum

$\frac{1}{2}$ teaspoon salt

1 egg, whisked (egg wash)

2 tablespoons caster (superfine) sugar, to sprinkle

APPLE FILLING

750 g (1 lb 11 oz) granny smith (or similar) apples, grated

225 g (8 oz) caster (superfine) sugar

juice of 1 lemon

2 tablespoons dark rum

$\frac{1}{2}$ tablespoon ground cinnamon

This is a classic Croatian cake (or kolač as we say) and can be prepared for any occasion – as a dessert after Sunday lunch, or to have along with a cup of steaming Turkish coffee and a gossip session with your friends. You don't have to stick to the apple filling either; other popular variations include maraska sour (morello) cherries or walnuts. This cake is prepared in all parts of Croatia and I have to say I really do love it, no matter what the occasion. The sweet and sour flavour of the apple and the crumbly texture of the pastry work their delicious magic on the taste buds. It also keeps well for a number of days. Cut the cake up into squares and serve with caramel sauce and vanilla ice cream, or serve it on its own just sprinkled with sugar.

To make the apple filling, sauté the apple and sugar in a saucepan over high heat for 5 minutes. Add the lemon juice, rum and ground cinnamon.

Sift the flour and baking powder into a bowl.

Using an electric mixer, beat the butter and sugar until pale. Add the egg and lemon zest and beat on high until the mixture is pale and fluffy in texture. Fold in the flour, baking powder, rum and salt. Work the mixture into a dough but do not work it for too long. Refrigerate the dough for 1 hour.

Preheat the oven to 190°C (375°F).

Divide the dough in half, sprinkle with flour and roll out each half to fit a 15 × 20 cm (6 × 8 in) baking dish or tray. Line the dish with baking paper. The dough should be 1–2 cm (½–¾ in) thick.

Put one layer of dough in the dish and bake for 10 minutes. Remove from the oven, spread the filling over the top and cover with the remaining dough. Brush with the egg wash and sprinkle with caster sugar. Prick the top of the dough with a fork and bake until golden brown. Serve hot or cold, cut into squares.

# Dried fig cake

*Torta od suhih smokava*

SERVES 4

2 tablespoons
breadcrumbs, plus
1 tablespoon extra

30 ml (1 fl oz) prošek
(Dalmatian fortified
wine) or port

150 g (5½ oz) dried figs

5 eggs, separated

170 g (6 oz/¾ cup) caster
(superfine) sugar

70 g (2½ oz) almonds,
finely chopped (or ground
in a food processor)

pinch of ground cloves

1 teaspoon ground
cinnamon

50 g (1¾ oz) unsalted
butter, for greasing

sour (morello) cherry
jam (or blueberry
or strawberry)

slivered almonds, to serve

caster (superfine) sugar,
to serve

**Along the Croatian coast, figs are very common fruit trees in gardens. Most people dry their own figs to enjoy them year round. As a result, there are many cake and biscuit recipes in Croatia that include this ingredient. They are even put in rakija (a Croatian fruit brandy) and made into a lovely liqueur called smokovača. This cake contains some breadcrumbs, but you can substitute these with some extra crushed almonds instead to make it gluten free.**

In a bowl, soak the breadcrumbs in the prošek. Dice one-third of the figs.

Using an electric mixer, beat the egg yolks with the caster sugar for 20–30 minutes on high speed. Add the almonds, the diced figs, the ground cloves, cinnamon and breadcrumbs soaked in prošek, and mix well with a rubber pastry spatula.

Using an electric mixer, beat the egg whites until firm peaks, then fold this into the other mixture gently with a spatula.

Preheat the oven to 160°C (320°F).

Grease a 20 cm (8 in) round cake tin with the butter and sprinkle with 1 tablespoon of breadcrumbs. Pour the cake mixture into the tin and bake for about 45 minutes. The cake is ready when a skewer inserted in the centre comes out clean. When the cake is cooked, let it cool for a while in the tin.

Cut the cake in half, horizontally, spread the sour cherry jam on top of the bottom layer and cover with the top layer.

Slice the remaining figs. To serve, place the sliced figs around the edge of the cake and sprinkle the centre with some slivered almonds and caster sugar.

# Poppy seed cake

*Makovnjača*

SERVES 6

DOUGH

15 g ($\frac{1}{2}$ oz) fresh yeast or
4 g ($\frac{1}{4}$ oz) dried yeast

150 ml (5 fl oz) warm milk

1 tablespoon caster
(superfine) sugar

75 g (2$\frac{3}{4}$ oz) unsalted butter

1 egg, plus 1 egg yolk

2 tablespoons extra-virgin
olive oil

350 g (12$\frac{1}{2}$ oz/2$\frac{1}{3}$ cups) plain
(all-purpose) flour

50 g (1$\frac{3}{4}$ oz) brown sugar

1 tablespoon baking powder

zest of 1 orange

zest of 1 lemon

$\frac{1}{2}$ teaspoon salt

1 vanilla bean

1 egg, whisked (egg wash)

FILLING

15–200 ml ($\frac{1}{2}$–7 fl oz) milk

150 g (5$\frac{1}{2}$ oz) caster
(superfine) sugar

300 g (10$\frac{1}{2}$ oz/2 cups) poppy
seeds, ground

30 ml (1 fl oz) dark rum

30 g (1 oz) unsalted butter

pinch of ground cinnamon

pinch of freshly grated
nutmeg

zest of 1 lemon

1 tablespoon honey

1 egg, beaten

**Poppy seed cake served with Turkish coffee is Croatia's version of high tea. It's the perfect combination for social gatherings, perfumed by the strong scent of the coffee. When you're attending a Croatian high tea, it's important to share your views on politics, fashion and all the other important subjects in life. I love the intriguing interplay between the sweet and bitter flavours of this cake.**

Mix the yeast into half the warm milk. Add 1 tablespoon flour and the sugar and whisk well to combine. Cover with plastic wrap and leave in a warm place for about 20 minutes.

In a saucepan over low heat, melt the butter in the remaining warm milk. Do not allow it to come to the boil.

In a bowl, mix the egg and egg yolk with the olive oil.

In another bowl, place the flour, brown sugar, baking powder, orange and lemon zest and salt. Split the vanilla bean, scrape out the seeds and add these to the bowl also. Mix to combine, then make a well in the centre of the dry ingredients and add the wet ingredients – the yeast mixture, the milk and butter and the egg and oil.

Using an electric mixer (or by hand), work the dough until it is smooth. Cover the dough with a cloth and leave in a warm place for about 1 hour to prove. You can now prepare the filling.

For the filling, put the milk and sugar in a saucepan over medium heat and stir until the sugar has dissolved. Add the poppy seeds and all the other ingredients, except the egg, and cook for 3–5 minutes until the mixture thickens. Remove the pan from the heat and mix in the egg. If the mixture is too thick add a little more milk.

When the dough has doubled in size, transfer it to a floured work surface and roll it out to a thickness of 5 mm (¼ in). Spread the poppy seed mixture over it evenly and roll up the dough, like a swiss (jelly) roll, into a roulade. Place on a baking tray lined with baking paper, cover with a cloth and leave to prove for another hour.

Preheat the oven to 180°C (350°F).

Prick the roulade with a fork, glaze with the egg wash and bake for 50–60 minutes. After about 20–30 minutes, cover it with aluminium foil to prevent it from becoming too dark. When cooked, cover with a cloth and allow to cool before serving.

# Almond cake from Makarska

*Torta makarana*

SERVES 6

DOUGH

400 g (14 oz/2⅔ cups)
plain (all-purpose) flour

3 egg yolks

200 g (7 oz) butter,
softened

2 tablespoons caster
(superfine) sugar

zest of 1 lemon

pinch of salt

30 ml (1 fl oz) maraschino
liqueur

FILLING

1 kg (2 lb 3 oz) almonds

15 eggs, separated

1 kg (2 lb 3 oz) icing
(confectioners') sugar

1 vanilla bean, split and
seeds scraped

zest and juice of 1 lemon

zest and juice of 1 orange

1 nutmeg, freshly grated

50 ml (1¾ fl oz)
maraschino liqueur, plus
extra to glaze

50 ml (1¾ fl oz)
amaretto liqueur

•

**Makarska is a small town not far from my hometown, Split. It is nestled in a small bay under the Biokovo Mountains. You will find some of the best beaches in the world around Makarska. The contrast of the pristine blue sea and white pebbles on the beaches, with the green pine trees and a huge mountain range in the background, makes it a very special place. If you visit Makarska, you have to taste this cake to complete the experience.**

For the dough, sift the flour into a mixing bowl. Add the egg yolks, softened butter, sugar, lemon zest, salt and maraschino. Work into a smooth dough. Set aside in the refrigerator for 30 minutes.

For the filling, preheat the oven to 180°C (350°F).

Put the almonds on a baking tray and roast them in the oven for about 10 minutes. Allow to cool, then blitz them in a food processor to a coarse crumb.

In a large bowl, using an electric mixer, beat the egg yolks and sugar until smooth and pale in colour. Add the vanilla seeds, ground almonds, lemon and orange zest and juice, nutmeg, maraschino and amaretto. In another large bowl, beat the egg whites to soft peaks with an electric mixer. Gently fold into the almond filling until smooth.

Preheat the oven to 180°C (350°F). Grease a 15–20 cm (6–8 in) round cake tin or six 8 cm (3¼ in) individual fluted tart tins.

On a floured work surface, roll the dough out to a thickness of 5 mm (¼ in) and use it to line the inside of the cake tin. If you are making individual cakes, use a pastry cutter to cut out discs of pastry that are 10 cm (4 in) in diameter. You will have some dough left over. Roll this out to the same thickness and cut it into 1.5 cm (½ in) strips, the width of the cake tin.

Put the almond filling into the pastry-lined tin then cover with the pastry strips in a criss-cross pattern, so you have 1 cm (½ in) diamond-shaped gaps between them. Bake for 35–45 minutes until golden. Brush with the maraschino liqueur. Cover with a clean cloth and leave to cool before serving.

# Dubrovnik crème caramel

*Dubrovačka rožata*

SERVES 8

6 eggs

280 g (10 oz) caster (superfine) sugar

1 litre (34 fl oz/4 cups) milk

zest of 2 lemons

2 tablespoons maraschino liqueur

1 teaspoon natural vanilla extract

whipped cream, to serve (optional)

**Rožata is one of Dubrovnik's most famous dishes. There are similar dishes in Italy, France and Spain and everyone claims it as their own original recipe. For me though, there is only one original rožata (crème caramel) and it's made in Dubrovnik. I still recall my Teta (Aunt) Mare from Get (an inner-city suburb in the town of Split) and her rožata. Somehow, every time we visited her she had a slice of this delicious dessert waiting for me. Now, whenever I make rožata (and that's almost every day, since it's on my restaurant's menu), I remember Teta Mare and her perfect rožata.**

**You will need eight 200 ml (7 fl oz) aluminium moulds, or one large mould. If you are using one single large mould, you will have to cut the rožata up when it has cooked and cooled.**

In a freestanding electric mixer, beat the eggs and 180 g (6½ oz) of the sugar until creamy and pale. Add the milk, lemon zest, maraschino and vanilla, and mix well.

In a saucepan, caramelise the remaining sugar and pour the caramel into the bottom of the moulds so it's about 3 mm (⅛ in) thick. Let the caramel cool.

Preheat the oven to 150°C (300°F).

Pour the milk and egg mixture into the moulds. Cook the rožata in a bain-marie – a large roasting tin filled with enough hot water to come halfway up the sides of the moulds – for about 40 minutes or until set. Be careful not to overcook the rožata – occasionally shake a mould to check if the mixture has set. It should be wobbly but still compact. Also, the mixture should not rise, it should only set.

Remove the rožata from the oven and transfer to the refrigerator for a few hours. Remove from the refrigerator and gently cut around the edges of the tin with a knife. Turn the rožata out onto a plate, and let the caramel liquid from the bottom of the mould fill the plate around the dessert. Serve the rožata chilled, topped with whipped cream, if using.

# Easter bread
## *Sirnica*

### SERVES 8

1 kg (2 lb 3 oz/6⅔ cups) plain (all-purpose) flour

50 g (1¾ oz) fresh yeast

250 g (9 oz) caster (superfine) sugar

100 g (3½ oz) unsalted butter, softened

100 g (3½ oz) lard

8 eggs (10 if they are small), separated

1 teaspoon salt

5 drops rose extract

20 ml (¾ fl oz) maraschino liqueur

20 ml (¾ fl oz) dark rum

250 ml (8½ fl oz/1 cup) milk, warmed

zest of 2 lemons

zest of 2 oranges

2 eggs, whisked (egg wash)

100 g (3½ oz) white sugar cubes, roughly broken

icing (confectioners') sugar, for dusting (optional)

**Sirnica is one of the most important dishes for the Catholic Easter in Dalmatia. We take this bread, coloured eggs, salt, spring onions (scallions) and wine to be blessed in church at the midnight mass before Easter. On Easter day we eat all this blessed food and wine for a breakfast. Even in Australia my family keeps this tradition every year.**

Sift the flour into a mixing bowl.

In another bowl, mix the yeast into a paste with a few tablespoons of warm milk. Add 1 tablespoon of sugar and 60 g (2 oz) of the flour, mix well and let it prove for 30 minutes. When the yeast mixture is ready it will foam and double in size. Add 100 g (3½ oz/⅔ cup) of the flour and mix it into a dough. Let it prove overnight.

The following morning, using a freestanding electric mixer, mix the softened butter and lard with the remaining sugar, adding the egg yolks one by one, mixing well after each addition. Mix in the salt, rose extract, maraschino, rum, warm milk and lemon and orange zest. Mix all the ingredients well.

In a separate bowl, beat the egg whites into soft peaks and mix them into the other ingredients gently with a spatula.

Put the yeast dough and egg mixture into a bowl with the remaining flour and mix into a smooth dough. Leave it to rest in a warm place, not hotter than 30°C (85°F), to prove for about 3–4 hours.

Cut some baking paper into round 15 cm (6 in) shapes. Cut the dough into four pieces and form round breads. Place them on the baking paper and cover with a wool blanket. Leave in a warm place for 3–4 hours.

When the breads are doubled in size, uncover them and let them dry for 30 minutes. Crush the sugar cubes in a tea towel (dish towel) with a mallet or pestle, until coarse.

Preheat the oven to 180°C (350°F).

Cut three (not too deep) cuts in the bread using a knife, brush with the egg wash and sprinkle with the broken sugar. Bake in the oven for 30 minutes. Cool and dusting with icing sugar, if using, before serving.

# Pepper biscuits from Hvar
## *Paprenjaci hvarski*

SERVES 8

500 g (1 lb 2 oz/3⅓ cups) plain (all-purpose) flour

1 egg

200 g (7 oz) lard, plus extra for greasing

250 g (9 oz) honey

70 g (2½ oz) caster (superfine) sugar

120 g (4½ oz) walnuts, finely chopped, plus extra walnut halves for decoration

20 g (¾ oz) baking powder

1 teaspoon ground cinnamon

2 pinches of ground cloves

zest of ½ orange

pinch of salt

pinch of finely ground pepper

2 eggs, whisked (egg wash)

•

**The island of Hvar is one of the most beautiful in Croatia. Almost every time I go to Croatia, Hvar is one of the places I visit. You can buy these indigenous cookies on the island as a souvenir to take home as a sweet memory from this wonderful place.**

Sift the flour into a mixing bowl. Add the egg, lard, honey, sugar, walnuts, baking powder, cinnamon, cloves, orange zest, salt and pepper. Work the mixture into a dough.

Preheat the oven to 220°C (430°F). Grease a baking tray.

Transfer the dough to a lightly floured work surface and roll it out to a thickness of 5 mm (¼ in).

Using different cookie cutters, cut the dough into a variety of shapes. Prick the biscuits with a fork and decorate them with a walnut half. Put the biscuits on the baking tray, brush with the egg wash and bake for 10–15 minutes until golden brown. Turn them out onto a wire rack to cool. The biscuits will keep stored in an airtight container for up to 2 months.

# Rafioli

*Sweets from Trogir*

SERVES 8

1 egg

50 g (1¾ oz) caster
(superfine) sugar, for
sprinkling

DOUGH

700 g (1 lb 9 oz/4⅓ cups)
plain (all-purpose) flour

6 egg yolks

200 g (7 oz) butter

100 g (3½ oz) caster
(superfine) sugar

1 vanilla bean, split and
seeds scraped

200 ml (7 fl oz) milk

zest of 1 orange

FILLING

500 g (1 lb 2 oz) roasted
almonds, finely chopped

500 g (1 lb 2 oz) caster
(superfine) sugar

zest of ½ lemon

zest of ½ orange

½ vanilla bean, split and
seeds scraped

¼ teaspoon freshly grated nutmeg

100 g (3½ oz) butter

100 g (3½ oz) lard

50 g (1¾ oz) dark chocolate,
grated

50 ml (1¾ fl oz) dark rum

¼ teaspoon ground cinnamon

50 ml (1¾ fl oz) maraschino
liqueur

6 egg whites

**Trogir is one of the pearls of the Adriatic. It's an enchanting medieval town built on a small island. I love to visit Trogir every time I go back home to Split. Its small, narrow streets, constructed from white marble, are dotted with eateries we call 'konoba' in Dalmatia. They offer fresh fish and good Dalmatian wine. You can also find some great rafioli there to finish your meal.**

Mix the dough ingredients together in a large bowl until you have a nice, smooth, compact dough. Rest for 30 minutes in the refrigerator.

For the filling, put all the ingredients, except the egg whites, in a bowl and mix together well.

Using an electric mixer, beat the egg whites to soft peaks. Gently fold the whipped egg whites into the filling mixture.

Remove the dough from the refrigerator and, on a floured work surface, roll out the dough to a thickness of 2 mm (⅛ in). Using a 6 cm (2½ cm) cookie cutter or a glass, cut out rounds from the dough. Re-roll the excess dough and cut again.

Spoon 1 tablespoon of filling into the centre of each circle of dough. Fold and shape the rafioli into half-moon shapes using your fingers and seal the edges with a fork. Make sure there are no air pockets in the pastry.

Preheat the oven to 165°C (330°F).

Whisk the egg and, using a pastry brush, cover the rafioli with the egg wash, then sprinkle with the caster sugar. Bake for about 20 minutes until golden brown. Cool on a wire rack. They will keep for a few weeks in an airtight container.

# Sweet crispy bread
## *Škanjate*

MAKES 1.5 KG (3 LB 5 OZ)

30 g (1 oz) fresh yeast
1.5 kg (3 lb 5 oz/10 cups) plain (all-purpose) flour
125 g (4½ oz) caster (superfine) sugar
250 ml (8½ fl oz/1 cup) vegetable oil
1 teaspoon salt
125 ml (4 fl oz/½ cup) milk

**Škanjate are small sweet, crispy breads that are very close to my heart. My grandmother Tomica always had plenty of them in the pantry. She would take great care baking them, slicing them and then drying them in the oven. Her house always had that sweet smell. They can keep for weeks in an airtight container and they are great dipped in tea, coffee or prošek, Dalmatian fortified wine – if you don't have prošek, any sweet wine will do.**

The night before you want to make the škanjate, mix the yeast with 25 g (1 oz) of the flour, 25 ml (1 fl oz) water and a pinch of the sugar in a bowl and let it prove overnight at room temperature.

The following day, sift the remaining flour into a large bowl. Make a well in the centre and add the oil, remaining sugar, salt, milk, 125 ml (4 fl oz/½ cup) of water and the yeast mix.

Work into a smooth dough for about 10–15 minutes. Divide the dough into bread rolls – the size depends on your baking tray, but approximately 10–15 cm (4–6 in) in length and 5 cm (2 in) wide. Grease the baking tray with oil, place the rolls next to each other and mould them into loaf shapes. Leave to prove until doubled in size, about 1–2 hours. It's okay if the breads have expanded and are touching each other.

Preheat the oven to 180°C (350°F). Bake the loaves until cooked, about 20–30 minutes. Cool them on a wire rack covered with a tea towel (dish towel). When the loaves are cool, cut them into 1 cm (½ in) slices and dry in a 160°C (320°F) oven until just golden brown, about 10 minutes. Store in an airtight container and they will keep for weeks.

# Sour cherry liqueur

*Liker od višnje*

MAKES 2 LITRES (68 FL OZ)

2 kg (4 lb 6 oz) sour
(morello) cherries, washed
1 kg (2 lb 3 oz) caster
(superfine) sugar
2 vanilla beans
1 litre (34 fl oz/4 cups)
grappa

**Croatians love their liqueurs and use them both for social occasions and also home remedies. They believe, although it is not medically proven, that each liqueur has its own purpose. My grandmother said sour cherry liqueur was good for the brain, curing nervousness, anxiety and stress. And even if the health benefits are nothing more than a placebo effect, you might as well give it a try!**

Put the sour cherries in a sterilised 3 litre (101 fl oz/12 cup) glass jar with the sugar, vanilla beans and grappa. Give it a stir and leave in a sunny place for 40 days. After 40 days, strain the liqueur into glass bottles. It will keep for years and gets better with age.

# Honey liqueur

*Medica*

MAKES 2.5 LITRES
(85 FL OZ)

1 kg (2 lb 3 oz) honey
1 litre (34 fl oz/4 cups)
grappa, or to taste

**This is a very popular liqueur in Croatia. Once made, keep it in a cool place, such as a pantry. You can drink it straight away, but the more you age it, the better it gets. It's great served with all kind of desserts. Also it is drunk in Croatia when one has a chest cough and cold – the honey is great for the lungs, and the grappa will take care of everything else.**

In a saucepan bring 500 ml (17 fl oz/2 cups) water to the boil. Once it has reached boiling point, remove from the heat and dissolve the honey in the water. Then start gradually adding the grappa, tasting as you go, to see how strong you want the flavour. Use as much of the grappa as you like. Allow to cool completely then strain into glass bottles. It will keep for years.

# Green walnut liqueur

*Orahovica*

MAKES 1 LITRE (34 FL OZ)

12 green walnuts
(get these from a walnut
tree before they ripen)

1 lemon

1 orange

300 g ($10\frac{1}{2}$ oz/$1\frac{3}{4}$ cups)
caster (superfine) sugar

2 vanilla beans

1 litre (34 fl oz/4 cups)
grappa

**You can use this liqueur in cocktails as an aperitif, and it makes a great digestive after a meal. Orahovica is also known to cure stomach pains. When I was a child my grandmother would give me a sip of this when I had a stomach ache. Almost every Croatian house will have this ancient remedy on hand.**

Wash the green walnuts wearing gloves (otherwise your hands will be black) then cut them into quarters.

Wash the lemon and the orange and peel the skin off with a small knife, making sure not to include any white pith.

Put the green walnuts in a sterilised 3 litre (101 fl oz/12 cup) glass jar with the sugar, lemon peel, orange peel and vanilla beans, then cover with grappa. Stir well, seal the jar and keep in a sunny place for 40 days. After 40 days, strain the liqueur into glass bottles. It will keep for years and gets better with age.

# Carob liqueur

*Liker od rogača*

MAKES 1 LITRE (34 FL OZ)

5–6 carob pods

300 g ($10\frac{1}{2}$ oz/$1\frac{3}{4}$ cups)
caster (superfine) sugar

1 litre (34 fl oz/4 cups)
grappa

**Around our olive grove in Croatia there are many carob trees. They have been planted to protect the olives from cold northerly winds and protect us when we pick the olives during the harvest in early winter. There are many uses for carob, which is sometimes called poor man's chocolate as it does have a bit of a chocolate/coffee flavour. When it is ripe, it can keep for months due to its antibacterial properties. Carob, dried figs and grappa are some of the offerings to be found on the table when you visit a Dalmatian home.**

Split the carob pods in half and put them in a sterilised 2 litre (68 fl oz/ 8 cup) glass jar. Add the sugar and grappa and leave in a sunny place for 40 days. After 40 days, strain the liqueur into glass bottles. It will keep for years and gets better with age.

# Acknowledgements

•

I dedicate this book to my beautiful wife Marijana for all her love, support and patience.

I love my native home Croatia and I have been working very hard to promote Croatian culture here in Australia. In 2004, my brother Natko Kuvačić and I opened Dalmatino, our restaurant in Port Melbourne. It has been a great success for over 12 years. This cookbook is the product of our passion and love for Dalmatian cuisine.

I want to thank my friend Slavica Habjanovic, who was the alfa and omega of this project.

Thank you to the team at Hardie Grant. First, to Jane Willson, who saw the potential in this project, to Andrea O'Connor who made much of the hard work look so easy, and to Emily O'Neill, for her fresh and original design.

Thank you to Leesa O'Reilly for bringing all the grace and beauty to our food photos, and to Ariana Klepac for adding sense to my recipes.

# About
# the author

•

Ino Kuvačić was born in Split, Croatia where he studied to become a chef.

In 1997, he moved to Australia where he worked in some of the country's most iconic restaurants, including Grossi Florentino in Melbourne, and Otto in Sydney.

In 2004, his long-time dream of owning a restaurant came true, and he opened Dalmatino in Port Melbourne with his brother, Natko Kuvačić.

Since then, Ino has been bringing the flavours of his beloved Croatia to Melbourne's restaurant scene. This is his first book.

# Index

•

First published in 2017 by Hardie Grant Books,
an imprint of Hardie Grant Publishing

Hardie Grant Books (Melbourne)
Building 1, 658 Church Street
Richmond, Victoria 3121

Hardie Grant Books (London)
5th & 6th Floors
52–54 Southwark Street
London SE1 1UN

hardiegrantbooks.com

A Cataloguing-in-Publication entry is available from the catalogue
of the National Library of Australia at www.nla.gov.au

*Dalmatia*
ISBN 978 1 74379 255 1

Publishing Director: Jane Willson
Managing Editor: Marg Bowman
Project Editor: Andrea O'Connor
Editor: Ariana Klepac
Design Manager: Mark Campbell
Designer: Emily O'Neill
Photographers: Chris Middleton and Ino Kuvačić
Stylist: Leesa O'Reilly
Production Manager: Todd Rechner
Production Coordinator: Rebecca Bryson

Colour reproduction by Splitting Image Colour Studio

Printed in China by 1010 Printing International Limited

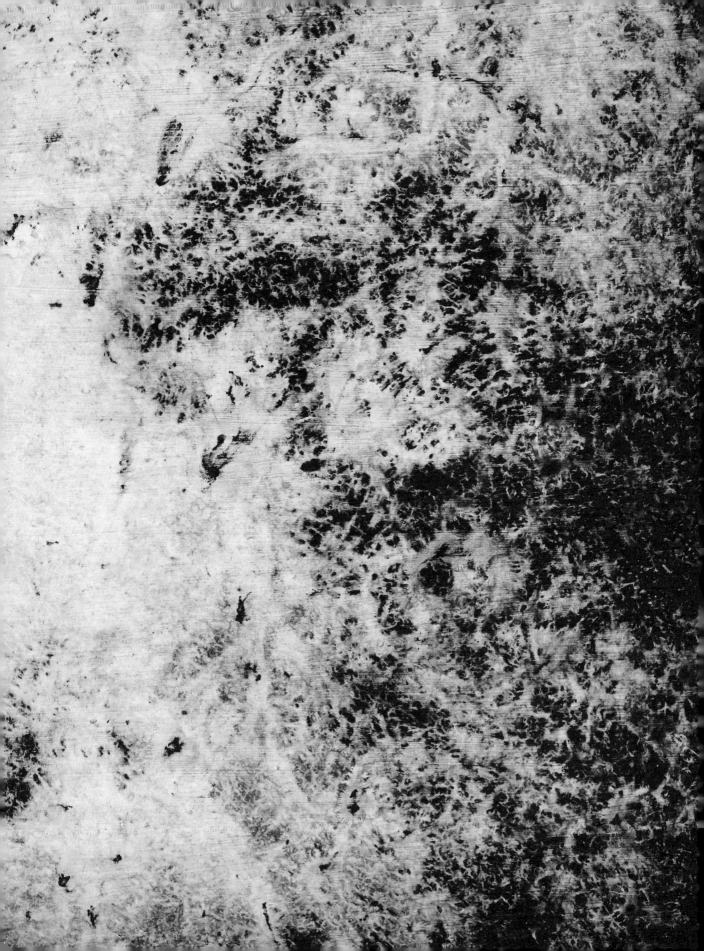